Changemaker

*50 tried and tested ways
to change the world*

AYESHA S. RATNAYAKE

Changemaker

For my mother and father,
who made me believe everything is possible.

"Who shall set a limit to the influence of a human being?"
Ralph Waldo Emerson

CONTENTS

THE WORLD NEEDS YOU

"Don't pretend that this world is equal – it's not.
The question is: What are you going to do about it?"
Dame Emma Thompson

A few years ago, I was the 29-year-old CEO of a technology firm and had recently raised hundreds of thousands of dollars to take my company forward. But I couldn't shake the idea that I was destined for something different. As impressive as people found my job and title, I knew I had the capacity and the responsibility to do something far more meaningful. So I quit my job without a clear plan. In a few years, I had a bestselling self-help book which has impacted the lives of thousands of people worldwide, and started a non-profit providing free educational resources to children around the country. Today, I feel I am living my purpose.

As an idealist, I am not alone. Around the world, many people come up against the problems of the world – global warming, poverty, discrimination, animal cruelty – and they take it upon themselves to help tackle those problems. Some of them make huge waves in the process, transforming the lives of hundreds, thousands and even millions. I believe that more of us can be like them.

Your passion to build a better world is the spark that can set off a fiery movement of change. History is bursting with examples of individuals and small groups who have kicked off major movements and sent the world in a new direction. Throughout this book, you will find stories of

1

people who have sparked serious changes. Some of them you may not have heard of, while others are well known. All have made incredible change. But every one of these people started out as an average person with passion – passion for building a better world. Just like you.

If a rap video can help factory workers in India, if an eight-year-old can secure clean water for her city, if an individual's plastic-free promise can be adopted by millions… what can you and I do to change this world?

Changemaker tells the stories of ordinary people who went on to make an extraordinary difference in the lives of others by acting from the heart. More importantly, it compiles the techniques adopted by these changemakers so that you too can use their methods to make an impact. Find out how a group of people with disabilities brought New York City to a standstill, how an 11-year-old Kenyan's invention is making peace between humans and wild animals, and how a 15-year-old invented a test to save cancer patients.

Use *Changemaker* as a guidebook for positive change – whether you have only a few minutes available today to do good or you want to dedicate your life to creating a more wonderful world.

The world needs you to care. Because there is so much that still needs to change. And *you* can make change happen. Let's get started.

CHOOSE YOUR MISSION

"Our deepest fear is not that we are inadequate.
Our deepest fear is that we are powerful beyond measure."
Marianne Williamson

There are so many problems in the world – from child poverty to global warming to racism. So many areas that need to be addressed. What is it that *you* would like to work on? Is there a particular cause that you are extremely passionate about? Or is there a wide range of causes that you would love to support? In considering how you want to make an impact, you have a lot of options. Let's explore them.

You can champion one cause

Chandima Rajapatirana was diagnosed with autism at the age of four. Unable to speak and communicate his needs, thoughts and feelings, he lived in what he describes as 'a silent abyss' until the age of 18. He listened to so-called experts tell his parents to put him in an institution, wanting to shout 'No!' yet unable to form the word. Thankfully, his mother believed in his intellect. She read to him constantly, and when she finally found a way for him to communicate by spelling on a keyboard, he emerged with a rich and vibrant vocabulary. Today, Chandima is an award-winning author and published poet whose story has appeared in TIME magazine and whose film poem has been screened at the United Nations headquarters.

Chandima decided to devote his life to giving voices to other non-speaking individuals. He and his mother started the EASE Foundation in Sri Lanka, an organisation dedicated to creating productive, stimulating lives for people with disabilities. He is committed to the cause of providing free and age-appropriate education to what he calls his 'tribe' – individuals with disabilities, many of whom travel from all over the island to benefit from his training.

Like Chandima, is there a particular cause that you have a personal connection with or that lights a fire in you? Perhaps it is something that you have had first-hand experience with. Maybe you have faced poverty and want to give other children better lives? Perhaps, as a female, you are especially interested in advocating for the rights of girls? Or perhaps you have always loved animals and want to make their welfare your priority? If there is a specific cause that resonates with you, you can make it your mission.

You can consider reach

When Scottish born William MacAskill was 15 years old, he learnt that a lot of people were dying from AIDS. He resolved that, one day, he would become very rich and would give away half of his wealth.

After graduating from university, he and another graduate called Toby Ord started an organisation called Giving What We Can. Giving What We Can encourages people to pledge at least 10% of their income to charities which operate highly effectively – those charities which save the most lives with each donation. One of their recommended charities is the Against Malaria Foundation which saves lives by distributing two-dollar insecticide-treated mosquito nets in regions affected by the mosquito-borne disease malaria, which affects over 200 million a year.

Today, the Giving What We Can movement has nearly 10,000 members from around the world who have taken the pledge to donate at least 10% of their income to charity. William himself has kept his childhood vow and donates over 50% of his income to causes that research suggests benefit the greatest number of people.

Research shows that some causes can benefit a larger number of individuals than others, and you may wish to give your time and attention to such causes. For example, the same amount of money (about USD 40,000) that could be used to fund the training of a single guide dog for a blind person in the USA may be used to restore the sight of hundreds or even thousands of people in the Global South who do not have access to simple trachoma surgeries.

Consider which causes can have the greatest potential impact numerically. They are typically causes which can serve a large number of people at a low cost, particularly those located outside the Global North (where there are, comparatively, many more support services). You can learn more about the types of causes that show effectiveness at thelifeyoucansave.org.

You can move upstream

When Melati and Isabel Wijsen were 12 and 10 years old respectively, they were curious about what they could do to make a difference, like the impressive people they had learnt about at school, from Lady Diana to Nelson Mandela. In 2013, the sisters started Bye Bye Plastic Bags, a campaign to ban plastic on the Indonesian island of Bali where they lived. Given that Indonesia was the world's second biggest plastic polluter after China, this was a big ask. They sought to get the government's attention and started a petition at the Bali airport, gathering 100,000 signatures in support of banning plastic in Bali.

Then, after learning about Mahatma Gandhi, the sisters decided to stage a hunger strike as he had done. (Note that the girls sought medical advice before planning their hunger strike. If you are considering using this tactic, be sure to do so as well!) They declared that they would not eat from dawn till dusk until the governor of Bali would meet them to discuss the plastic waste problem. Within 24 hours, they were escorted to the governor's home. With the girls' encouragement, he committed in writing to make Bali plastic bag free.

The Wijsen sisters continue to campaign for a plastic-free world, and have distributed over 10,000 educational booklets to schools, handed out over 16,000 alternative bags, organised Bali's biggest beach cleanup with 20,000 people, met numerous government leaders, delivered over 1,300 presentations worldwide (including at the United Nations), and expanded to more than 50 teams globally.

"The 23rd of June 2019 marks a big day in history for all of us activists, environmentalists and longtime supporters of the plastic-free movement. It is a day to celebrate as we welcome the long-awaited ban on single-use plastic bags, straws and polystyrene on our island home, Bali."
Melati and Isabel Wijsen

In the book 'Upstream: How to Solve Problems Before They Happen', Dan Heath describes how it can be a good idea to invest in proactive or upstream solutions more than reactive, downstream ones. To illustrate the value, he describes an imaginary scenario. You are walking along a river and see a child drowning, so you jump into the river and save the child. Five minutes later, you see another child and save that one too. At this point, he points out that the smartest solution would be to go upstream and identify the point where all these children are falling in the river and make a correction there. That way, the children won't need saving.

Instead of supporting causes that react after a problem has occurred (like collecting rubbish), perhaps you can support causes that prevent problems from occurring in the first place (like halting the production of single-use plastics). You might have a bigger impact this way.

You can do it all

Amariyanna Copeny lives in the city of Flint in Michigan, USA. When her city started providing its homes with toxic water containing dangerous levels of lead, she knew she had to take action. At the age of eight, Amariyanna wrote to President Obama to inform him about the crisis, leading him to visit Flint and approve USD 100 million in relief funds for the city. Amariyanna's efforts shone a national spotlight on the issue and earned her the nickname "Little Miss Flint". She also raised more than USD 250,000 and distributed over a million bottles of water. She then went on to partner with a company to raise over USD 600,000 to produce and distribute water filters to areas with improperly treated water.

While access to clean water is Amariyanna's primary cause, she also gets involved in many other areas. She works with an anti-bullying group and was national youth ambassador to the Women's March on Washington. She also supports underprivileged kids in her community by raising funds to provide backpacks and school supplies, toys during the festive season, and community events. She even initiated a book project to give local children books written by authors of colour, and inspired thousands of people from around the world to send supportive letters to kids in Flint.

Even if there is one primary cause you support or believe deserves the majority of your time and attention, you can always continue to support other causes as you go about living your life. You don't have to do so in big and dramatic ways – this can look as simple as carrying a reusable bag to the grocery store so you would not need a plastic one.

I sometimes hear people criticise action taken in support of a cause by stating "There are much bigger problems". However, support of one cause doesn't necessarily take anything away from any other cause – so even if it's true that there are "bigger" problems, that isn't a good reason not to champion any subject worth championing.

Remember, you don't have to stick to just one cause. You can organise a women's rights march while practicing veganism, wearing ethically-sourced clothes, writing letters to protest corporations' use of plastic packaging and donating money to effective charities. And of course, all the while, you can show respect to other humans, animals and the environment.

Select your cause(s)

Think about what cause(s) you would like to support. Ask yourself how you would like the world to be different. What would an ideal world look like to you? What do you feel would make the world a better place? What issues make you feel particularly sad or angry? What causes excite you? Mulling over these questions can help you identify the specific issues that are important to you.

The causes I'm most passionate about are those that prioritise equality and wellbeing. I realised how much these causes meant to me by noticing that the times I felt the most upset and angry were when I saw injustice play out. I've cried hot, angry tears when the life experiences of an individual from a minority community were dismissed, when a woman in a male-dominated home was denied agency, when a person with a disability was treated as unintelligent. I've found that issues related to equality and wellbeing are those I feel most deeply.

What are the causes that you want to support? Write down one or more here.

State your vision

Now, define your vision for the world in one sentence. For example, "A world where (the problem) does not exist." Write your vision here.

Do your research

Once you have identified the cause(s) that you would like to champion, begin to do your research. Educate yourself about each issue you care about, its major themes, milestones in its history, and the arguments made by advocates and opponents of the cause. Read books, watch documentaries, and follow credible news sources that provide information about the issue. If possible, conduct first-hand interviews.

Before my friends and I decided to create free educational content to tackle key issues such as child abuse and gender-based violence, we started by understanding the lived realities of people in our home country of Sri Lanka. We conducted interviews with individuals who faced these problems as well as people and organisations striving to solve them. We also read research papers and newspaper articles that discussed the issues we wanted to work on.

Today, we still refer the notes from those interviews and studies when we make decisions and create resources. By neatly organising and categorising our findings, we can easily look up statistics and anecdotes that support our work.

The better informed you are, the better equipped you will be to make a real difference. Here are some prompts to influence your research efforts.

What are the key facts that support the need to champion your cause(s)?

What are the major milestones in the history of your cause(s)?

What are the biggest barriers you can identify to making positive change in this area?

Your voice matters

You may be thinking 'If many people are working on my cause already, why does my voice matter?' It does. Sometimes people need to hear a message or see an action from a particular person or a particular perspective in order for it to resonate with them. The specific way you put something across, your background, geography and unique point of view can all make your message or action connect with someone in a way that no one else could before.

Can you think of ways in which your uniqueness helps you offer a fresh perspective on an issue or connect better with a particular group of people?

In addition, while efforts may be ongoing in one part of the world, another region may be neglected. Look out for the underserved areas. Where is your voice needed? This might be within a neglected geographical region, among an underserved community of people or simply where your voice and action would connect best.

Where do you think you would like to focus your efforts?

So, how can you begin to change the world? There are plenty of avenues open to you. In the upcoming chapters, we will explore some of the main routes for making change. We will also learn about individuals who have used these strategies successfully. What has worked for them may work for you too, so feel free to draw inspiration from their methods!

Keep your favourite cause area(s) in mind as you read, and think about how the strategies we discuss could be applied towards your preferred cause(s).

It's time to change the world.

SOCIAL ACTIVISM

"The world is not changed by people who sort of care."
Sally Hogshead

Social activism involves working with and influencing other people to create positive change in the world. You can become a catalyst in your community by raising awareness about important issues and being an active participant in the world around you. Here are some ways to do that.

Start a conversation

Great if you have skills in: Social intelligence, public speaking, research, negotiation, debate

Daryl Davis is an African American blues musician who has spent three decades befriending members of the white supremacist group the Ku Klux Klan (KKK), leading them to rethink their hatred.

After an encounter with a KKK member who was surprised by how much he enjoyed Daryl's music, Daryl decided to travel around the country to talk to Klan members. The more they got to know him, the more they saw through their own prejudices.

One encounter Daryl had was with a KKK member who insisted that all black people have violent genes. When Daryl pointed out that despite being black, he had never been violent, the Klansman smugly retorted that Daryl's violent gene was latent and yet to emerge. After a minute's thought, Daryl said "Well, we all know that all white people have a gene within them that makes them a serial killer." He asked the Klansman to name three black serial killers, and when he could not do it, Daryl rattled off the names of well-known white serial killers – Ted Bundy, Charles Manson, Jeffrey Dahmer, John Wayne Gacy.

When the Klansman insisted that he personally had never hurt anyone, Daryl suggested that his serial killer gene must be latent. "Well, that's stupid!" said the Klansman, to which Daryl agreed, while pointing out that it was no more stupid than what he had said to Daryl. The Klansman became very quiet, and five months later, he left the KKK based on that conversation. He handed his white Klan robes over to Daryl.

Over 30 years, Daryl convinced over 200 Klansmen to give up their robes. He keeps these robes in his home as a reminder of the impact he has made through the simple act of conversation.

Engaging in discussions with friends, family and peers can help raise awareness about social issues and create positive change. Having conversations about difficult topics can help break down barriers and promote understanding – try it at family gatherings, meetups with friends, and at your school or workplace.

For the best impact, study alternate views and be prepared with convincing data and anecdotes that support your perspective. Daryl studied deeply about the KKK before initiating his tour, coming to know as much or even more about the organisation as the people he spoke with. This won their respect and often helped him secure a second meeting.

Even a short conversation can change how people think for the rest of their lives. I have personally had brief encounters where I shared a controversial opinion, seemed to encounter resistance, yet later been surprised to hear from the other person that they had changed their behaviour based on the information I had shared. Speak up – you might have a bigger impact than you expect!

Write an email or letter

Great if you have skills in: Writing

When Witek Hebanowski was a local group coordinator for Amnesty International in Poland, he met a girl called Joanna at a festival. She told him how she had recently been in Africa, where 24-hour letter-writing events were organised to write protest letters to governments. Witek invited her to an Amnesty meeting. There, they decided to spend 24 hours writing letters of protest and to invite other groups to join in.

They told other Amnesty offices around the world about the concept – and started receiving photos of letter-writing events taking place all over – in Japan, Mongolia, even by Niagara Falls! Within a year, Write for Rights became a global Amnesty event. Ever since, millions of people have taken part in letter-writing events on or around Human Rights Day (December 10th). They write to the people whose freedoms are at risk to express solidarity, and to the authorities to demand justice.

And the letters work. To share one example, Burundian human rights defender Germain Rukuki was sentenced to 32 years in prison on bogus charges aimed at preventing his human rights work. People around the world took more than 435,000 actions on his behalf, writing letters, signing petitions, tweeting and emailing. In four years (instead of 32), he was reunited with his wife and three children.

"Write for Rights really does have a positive impact. Their support has made me come out of prison even more committed to defending human rights."
Germain Rukuki

One way of influencing the actions of those in power is by writing to them directly. If you would like to influence the decisions of politicians or to encourage them to prioritise certain issues on their agendas, you could try writing a letter or an email to them.

This simple approach suits many situations. You can write to companies, radio shows, or school principals! For example, you could confront a magazine about depicting groups of people in stereotypical ways, or encourage the CEO of a large company to switch to recyclable packaging of their products. A friend of mine goes one step further and collects the company's plastic packaging waste, then sends it back to them to emphasise the point!

For best effect, remember to keep your letter short (no more than one page), explain why the issue is important to you, be specific about the action you expect, verify the facts within, and request a response (don't forget to include your return address). Check the Template Toolkit at the back of this book to see a simple format for writing your own letter calling for action. If you do not receive a reply and the issue is not addressed, consider writing another letter or sending a copy of your letter to the local newspaper.

If you can inspire more people – for example, your whole class or group of friends – to write as well, you are likely to have a much greater impact. Share your letters on social media to encourage others in the community to support your efforts and to do the same. The more people you can encourage to act, the greater the chances that your letters will gain attention, so don't be shy about sharing your actions.

In addition, you can write letters to newspapers in order to draw attention to important issues. If your pieces are published, this can help you influence the community to change their perspectives on an issue or to adopt behaviours that positively contribute to a cause.

Also consider writing thank you letters to the changemakers (including people, politicians and corporations) that you are impressed with – it can provide them with the encouragement they need to keep fighting the good fight!

Make a call

Great if you have skills in: Social intelligence, public speaking, negotiation

In 2012, the United States government was set to introduce an act which would give the government license to shut down websites of their choosing on copyright claims. The CEO of the microblogging website Tumblr, David Karp, recognised this as a threat to digital democracy, and he and his team mulled over the best way to raise awareness.

In order to activate its audience, the Tumblr website demonstrated what censorship might look like by obscuring user-generated text, videos and images on its platform while inviting viewers to take a stand against online censorship.

The website partnered with Mobile Commons to provide a page where users could input their phone number and area code to automatically call their representative in Congress and voice their concerns about the bill. In a single day, over 87,000 calls were placed, with callers spending nearly 1,300 hours in total talking to representatives. More organisations followed Tumblr's lead, and eventually, over 400,000 calls were made to Congress. Within a day, so many senators had withdrawn their support that the act never came to pass.

> *"I commute a lot to work, so I have downtime.*
> *I have Bluetooth set up in my car and I just say, 'O.K., call Roy*
> *Blunt's D.C. office' every day now. That's my routine."*
> *Mikayla Dreyer, Missouri constituent*

If you can get hold of the contact numbers of people in authority, such as politicians and company heads, pick up your phone and give them a call. Getting phone numbers can be surprisingly easy using the Internet. Many countries have websites which collate the contact information of their parliamentarians and local government authorities

– check if yours is one of them. A phone call takes just a few minutes so it can be easily squeezed in while you reheat yesterday's leftovers or wait for the bus. It is also harder to ignore than emails and letters.

Tell your political representatives and company heads about the issues that are important to their constituents and customers, and what you hope to see them do about those issues. Do you want them to adjust their marketing practices, vote in favour of a cause, cease to sell a particular product, or co-sponsor a bill? Check the Template Toolkit at the back of this book to see a simple guideline for getting your message across quickly and with impact.

"I've written bills that became law because people called to complain about a particular issue I was unaware of."
Isaiah Akin, deputy legislative director in Oregon

Your call may help authorities realise that enough people care passionately about an issue for them to decide to prioritise it. Indeed, short of showing up in person (feel free to do that too!), making calls is reputed to be one of the most effective ways of petitioning government. One reason is that when crowds of people call in, this can make it difficult for the government/corporate office to attend to other work besides answering phones!

Make a declaration

Great if you have skills in: Leadership, social intelligence, public speaking, debate

Colin Kaepernick was a quarterback in the United States' National Football League (NFL). In 2016, when his country was rocked with protests against racial injustice and police brutality, he decided to take a public stand – by refusing to stand. When the national anthem was played before football games, instead of rising with his teammates, he knelt as an act of peaceful protest. He later told the media, "I am not going to stand up to show pride in a flag for a country that oppresses black people and people of colour. To me, this is bigger than football, and it would be selfish on my part to look the other way." His act sparked a nationwide conversation and inspired other athletes to join in solidarity.

Simply by making a public declaration of what you stand for, you can inspire others to reflect on their own principles. It allows you to live authentically, build trust among others, and be a catalyst for positive social change. What do you stand for?

Start a petition

Great if you have skills in: Research, writing, social media presence

When Amika George was 17 years old, she learnt that as many as one in ten girls in the United Kingdom were missing school because they could not afford menstrual hygiene products. Shocked by this, on a rainy Friday from her bedroom, she launched an online petition. The #FreePeriods campaign urged the British government to provide free period products to schools. It attracted nearly 200,000 signatures. Amika also staged a protest outside Downing Street, where the Prime Minister's residence is housed, and over 2,000 people participated.

The following year, the government set aside £1.5 million (nearly USD 2 million) to address the issue. But Amika felt this was not enough. She started crowdfunding the legal fees to push the government for a permanent solution. Thanks to Amika's efforts, the United Kingdom now provides free period products in every secondary school and college across England, supporting girls across the country in accessing their right to education.

> *"If you feel you want to do something, there's strength in numbers."*
> Amika George

Petitions can be a great way to get the attention of someone in power by demonstrating that a lot of people care about an issue, and that the politician, company or other authority's choices on the matter will affect their popularity.

When creating a petition, consider timing. If you can circulate your petition at a time when people are most engaged with an issue and passionate about it, it is likely to gain more traction. For example, when a controversial decision is made by the government, when the media has shined a spotlight on a problem, or when an incident occurs that highlights how critical an issue is. Online petitioning platforms like Change.org can help you circulate your petition rapidly and quickly gather signatures. You never know, your petition might even go viral! Check the Template Toolkit at the back of this book to see a simple format for preparing your own petition.

Start a protest

Great if you have skills in: Leadership, social intelligence, organising groups, planning and coordination, public speaking

Greta Thunberg is a Swedish environmental activist who has Asperger's syndrome. She learned about climate change when she was around 8 years old. On learning that livestock and airplanes are key greenhouse gas emitters, she adjusted her habits, becoming vegan and ceasing travel by plane. When Greta was 15, for nearly three weeks before the 2018 Swedish election, she missed school to sit in front of the parliament carrying a sign stating "Skolstrejk för Klimatet" (School Strike for Climate). On the first day she sat alone, but each day more and more people joined her. Soon, her story became international news.

After the Swedish election, Greta continued to miss classes on Fridays to strike. In doing so, she started the 'Fridays for Future' movement. Inspired by her actions, hundreds of thousands of students across the world also took part in Fridays for Future strikes.

Greta was invited to talk about climate change at forums around the world, including the World Economic Forum, European Parliament and before the French, Italian, United Kingdom and United States legislatures. Following her impassioned speech in 2019 at a United Nations climate event in New York City, millions participated in climate strikes in over 163 countries. Her influence was called "the Greta effect".

"We are striking because we have done our homework and they [the politicians] have not."
Greta Thunberg

Protests can be a very effective way of drawing attention to a cause. They can take many forms, including a strike or sit-in. Consider starting a protest to draw attention to the cause of your choice. Like Greta showed us, even a one-person protest can make a huge impact!

Decide what specific issue you want to draw attention to, and the best time and location to perform the protest. For example, you may wish to protest outside a particular government building, or at a time when a key event is taking place, for maximum impact and visibility.

To maximise participation and attention, spread the word about the protest, for example, using social media, flyers and by contacting organisations that share your cause. Social media can be a powerful tool for organising and mobilising large groups of people. For example, during the Arab Spring in 2011, social media played a key role. With tools like Facebook and Twitter, organisers were able to quickly disseminate information about where and when protests were happening, allowing people to join in and make their voices heard.

Make sure you know and comply with the legal requirements for protesting in the area of your choice. Assign people to take the lead on logistics, creating banners and signs, and coordinating with the media. Ensure everyone appreciates the importance of non-violence in holding a credible protest that many will feel comfortable supporting. Non-violent tactics can include singing, chanting, and holding signs and banners. Check the Template Toolkit at the back of this book to see sample banner slogans and campaign chants for a variety of causes. Then go forth and make your voice heard!

Judith Heumann was passionate about making her voice heard. As someone who had polio as a child and used a wheelchair, she was unfairly denied a license when she applied to become a teacher. The next year she started a disability rights group demanding laws to protect the rights of people with disabilities. Together with 50 of her peers, Judith staged a sit-in on the busy roads of New York City, stopping traffic by blocking the four roads of an intersection with individuals in wheelchairs shouting and carrying placards. The demonstration caught media attention. But it was only a start. Next, over 100 people with disabilities staged a sit-in at a government building for 28 days. When the phones in the building were cut off, deaf individuals used sign language to communicate with media outside.

On a hot March day, 60 protestors, including 8-year-old Jennifer Keelan, got out of their wheelchairs and crawled up the 83 steps of the United States Capitol Building. The protestors' goal was to ensure that Congress would pass an act to require accessibility of buildings and public and private transportation and outlaw discrimination in employment based on disability. Their powerful message made an impact. Today, the Americans with Disabilities Act has been in place for over 30 years, benefitting individuals with disabilities across the country.

Start a boycott

Great if you have skills in: Social intelligence, planning and coordination, organising groups, social media presence

Rosa Parks grew up in Montgomery at a time of segregation – when black people faced severe discrimination in voting, housing, employment, education and transportation. They were not even allowed to drink from many public water dispensers. Rosa knew this was all terribly unfair, and she and her husband were members of the National Association for the Advancement of Colored People (NAACP). In fact, Rosa was the secretary of the Montgomery chapter.

One day, after a long day of work, 42-year-old Rosa was returning home by bus when the driver insisted she give up her seat for a white passenger. She refused. Eventually, two police officers took her into custody. This was not the first time Rosa had taken a stand – 12 years before, she had refused to enter the bus from the back door (rather than the front door) and left altogether rather than give in.

This time, Rosa's simple act of courage was to trigger a movement. Word of her arrest spread fast. The local black community, led by 26-year-old Dr. Martin Luther King Jr., decided to boycott the local bus system. 35,000 flyers were sent out. Since about 70% of bus users were African American, this deeply cut into the revenue of the municipal bus system. The boycott lasted for over a year, until the Supreme Court ruled against bus segregation. The Montgomery Bus Boycott, as it came to be known, also inspired boycotts around the country of segregated restaurants, pools, and other public facilities.

*"I was not tired physically... No, the
only tired I was, was tired of giving in."*
Rosa Parks

Is there a company, product or service that you believe hurts society? For example, in several South Asian countries where there is a bias towards lighter skin tones, multinational companies advertise skin-whitening products. These advertisements fuel notions that people with lighter skin are more attractive and deserving. If you look around you, you will discover billion-dollar corporations that avoid paying taxes, companies that have made controversial political donations, and entities that are selling unhealthy items to vulnerable populations (did you know that more than 80% of the world's tobacco users live in low- and middle-income countries?).

Consider organising a boycott – a coordinated effort to stop using services or products until the entity that provides them changes its actions or policies. Put forward a clear set of demands or goals for the boycott, and reach out to your friends, family, and social media networks to mobilise others to resist buying from them or endorsing their products and services.

Conduct a march or parade

Great if you have skills in: Leadership, social intelligence, organising groups, planning and coordination, public speaking

In New York City in June 1970, a group of friends and LGBT activists, Craig Rodwell, Fred Sargeant, Ellen Broidy, Linda Rhodes and Brenda Howard decided to hold a march to commemorate the Stonewall Uprising that had occurred the previous year where LGBT individuals had fought back against police violence.

As they didn't have a police permit for the march, the organisers feared how they might be treated by authorities, and lessons in self-defense were provided to participants. The route of the march covered 50 city blocks from Greenwich Village to Central Park, and thousands of people showed up. Marches were also held in Chicago, Los Angeles and San Francisco that year, and provided inspiration for hundreds of Pride parades that continue to take place around the world.

Conducting a march or parade for social change can be a powerful and impactful way to advocate for a cause, raise awareness, and mobilise communities. The scale of such events attracts media and public attention and sends a strong collective message. Marches and parades also provide an opportunity to educate the public about a cause, while giving participants a strong sense of empowerment.

*"As my friend Jerry Hoose used to say about that year,
'we went from the shadows to sunlight'."*
Mark Segal, marshal of the first Pride march

Start a fundraiser

Great if you have skills in: Social intelligence, planning and coordination, social media presence

When Declan Cassidy's sister Amber left home due to drug addiction, his mother would drive around the streets looking for her, with Declan often in tow. Declan learnt that what many homeless individuals wanted most was socks. That's when, at 10 years old, he decided to start a fundraiser, 'Declan's Socks for the Streets'. In 2022, Declan's fundraiser passed out more than 20,000 pairs of socks to people living on the streets. It has now become an official non-profit and Amber, who has gotten clean and come home, serves on its board.

*"I want him to look at that person and see them as a person,
not a homeless person on the street."*
Jennifer Cassidy, Declan's mother

Actively raising funds for a cause is a great way to contribute. Identify what you hope to achieve, how much you intend to raise, over what time period, and how you will reach donors. You might choose to use online crowdfunding platforms to raise funds, or host fundraiser events such as an auction or benefit concert. Or you might simply use social media and email.

Before reaching out, develop a clear and compelling message with emotional appeal, and when you contact donors, be clear about how their funds will be used to benefit the cause. Check the Template Toolkit at the back of this book to see a simple format for spreading the word about your fundraiser.

Having a supportive team to help with fundraising efforts can multiply their impact, so enlist the help of your friends and family.

Start a donation drive

Great if you have skills in: Social intelligence, planning and coordination, social media presence

As a 10-year-old, Marley Dias was surprised to find that although the books she had at home featured black girls and diverse experiences, the books at her school did not reflect such a colourful world. "I was only able to read books about white boys and their dogs," she says. Marley complained to her mother about this and her mother asked what she was going to do about it.

Marley decided to start the #1000BlackGirlBooks campaign to collect and donate 1,000 books with black females playing the lead roles. She was initially uncertain about whether she could meet her goal, but the online community rallied to support her. Today, Marley's efforts have seen over 14,000 books distributed to schools, libraries and community organisations across the world. Marley even published her own book at age 13: 'Marley Dias Gets It Done: And So Can You'.

> *"My goal is to ensure that kids know that changing the world should not be something that feels imaginary, but something that you have the power to do today and always."*
> *Marley Dias*

Like Marley, consider conducting a donation drive. For example, you could collect stationery for kids in hospital; used computers, instruments or bicycles for disadvantaged neighbourhoods; books, games or seasonal decorations for children's homes; or pool toys for community pools. You can set up a single collection point, or for greater reach, set up multiple collection points at different locations. Use clear signage and spread the word using social media, flyers and word of mouth.

Start a campaign

Great if you have skills in: Social intelligence, planning and coordination, research, writing, social media presence, public speaking, negotiation

When Hong Kong born James Chen was in high school, he had the same priority as others his age – getting his driving license. But when he failed the eye test, he discovered that he had a vision problem. James had lived in Nigeria with his family from the ages of three to ten, and he had noticed that people there hardly wore glasses. It occurred to him that the lack of affordable access to eyecare could be holding back millions of people. So he started the 'Clearly' campaign. The goal of the campaign was to educate the public and world leaders and ultimately enable access to glasses for everyone in the world.

But several professionals told James that making customised eyecare accessible affordably was impossible. He finally gained traction when he began to frame the vision issue not as a healthcare issue but as one about sustainable development. He highlighted that if citizens could not see, they could not take part in the country's economy. This finally led institutions to sit up and pay attention, and in July 2021, the United Nations adopted its first resolution on vision.

> *"Probably the biggest contribution of the Clearly campaign was to really reframe the issue for the global community; for policy makers and government leaders."*
> *James Chen*

Creating broad public and institutional awareness of an issue through a campaign can be an important way to help the issue get the attention and action it deserves. Consider whom you need to reach with your campaign, what messages they need to receive and what mediums to use to reach them. As part of your campaign, you can study the issue thoroughly, meet with authorities to lobby them to take action, deliver educational presentations about the issue and be a voice for change.

Like James, be aware that how you frame the issue can make a big difference to how it is received. Evaluate the key priorities of the most valuable audiences you need to reach – how can you align your mission with what matters to them?

Create a community

Great if you have skills in: Social intelligence, organising groups, planning and coordination, social media presence

Emmeline Pankhurst grew up in a time when women in the United Kingdom were not allowed to vote in political elections. Both her parents believed and advocated that both women and men should have equal 'suffrage' (the right to vote). By the age of 20, Emmeline was working hard for women's right to vote.

In 1903, she founded the Women's Social and Political Union (WSPU). The WSPU organised fundraising events and demonstrations, and Emmeline travelled across the country speaking at rallies and activating a community of women. Ninety branches of the organisation were set up across the United Kingdom. London – where the government was located – was the main hub.

The Suffragetes (women campaigning for the right to vote) maintained a constant presence near government buildings, presenting petitions, calling out members of parliament and even chaining themselves to government buildings. They produced a weekly newspaper called Votes for Women, which had a circulation of over 20,000. They also organised events where over 60,000 Suffragetes carried banners across London. The demonstrations attracted 300,000 people to watch.

In 1928, the year of Emmeline Pankhurst's death, women in England, Wales and Scotland finally received the vote. Two years later, a statue of Emmeline was unveiled close to the Houses of Parliament by the prime minister in honour of her life's campaign.

In order to maximise your impact, consider creating a community to join in your cause-related efforts and embarking on projects as a group. For example, you might start a regular group to write compassionate letters to prisoners or invite friends to join you in visiting elders' homes. Or you could organise a done-in-a-day project where volunteers can contribute to a beach cleanup or other activity. You could also initiate a group to help the participants themselves, such as a community for people to practice meditation together to alleviate anxiety. Consider converting your project into a club or society that meets at regular intervals (e.g. weekly). You can use social media such as WhatsApp and Facebook groups to attract and engage with community members.

Speak on radio or TV

Great if you have skills in: Public speaking, writing, research, negotiation, debate

When COVID-19 hit the world, Larissa Thorne, an intensive care nurse in England, was terrified about going to work. She would wake up in the middle of the night thinking about the virus, and often worried about her father, a cancer patient, contracting coronavirus. Yet, she would strive to look after patients with the level of care that she imagined her parents would want to receive.

Despite her long and stressful days, she agreed to participate in BBC's radio programme 'Coronavirus - Stories from behind the mask', keeping a diary of her experiences on the frontlines and sharing it with radio listeners. Stories like hers provided a human perspective on the challenges faced by medical professionals, building public support and highlighting the vital need for healthcare infrastructure like personal protective equipment that was in short supply.

By making an appearance on radio or television, you have the opportunity to share your experiences and views about causes that matter. Consider reaching out to local programmes and offering to share your story. Craft an interesting proposal describing why the topic is timely and relevant to local audiences, and describe how you can provide a unique perspective.

Host a public debate

Great if you have skills in: Social intelligence, organising groups, planning and coordination, social media presence, research, writing, public speaking, negotiation, debate

In 1965, an important debate took place between two writers – James Baldwin and William Buckley Jr. The subject of the debate was 'The American Dream is at the expense of the American Negro', and it took place at a time when many Black Americans like James were still denied the right to vote. James agreed with the motion while William disagreed. William had shined on Yale University's debate team, but it was James' first time taking part in a formal debate. Each debater had 15 minutes to make their case in front of nearly 1,000 students at the University of Cambridge Union Society in the United Kingdom.

While both speakers displayed great talent, James' eloquent and persuasive delivery led him to win by a huge margin, 544 to 164. "I picked the cotton, and I carried it to the market," he said, "and I built the railroads under someone else's whip for nothing. For nothing." When he finished speaking, James received a standing ovation – something the narrating host declared he never before seen at the Union.

Hosting a public debate is an effective way to facilitate a dialogue between individuals or groups with differing opinions on a particular issue. Select a clear and specific topic with two or more opposing viewpoints. Then identify speakers who represent the different perspectives on the topic and have expertise in their respective fields. They should be people who can present their arguments clearly, concisely and persuasively.

Next, establish the format of the debate. There are several formats to choose from, including a traditional point-counterpoint format, a panel discussion, or a town hall-style meeting. The format should allow for equal time and opportunities for all speakers to present their arguments and respond to questions. Choose a venue that is accessible, quiet, and can fit the number of attendees you expect. It should also be a neutral location, such as a university auditorium or community centre. Promote the debate through social media, email marketing, flyers, word of mouth, etc.

Conduct an event

Great if you have skills in: Social intelligence, organising groups, planning and coordination, social media presence

Three friends from the island nation of Sri Lanka, Nabila Imtiaz, Mihitha Basnayake and Ayesha Ratnayake (yes, that's me!) were determined to help address the gender-based violence, child abuse, unplanned pregnancies, menstrual health issues, discrimination, and more, that they kept hearing and reading about in the news. They decided that education was the most sustainable route to long-term change. So they began designing and delivering age-appropriate educational workshops to teach children about bodies and boundaries, gender equality, reproductive health, menstrual health, disability, and more. They were delighted by the responses to their workshops, knowing that these events could change the lives of the youth who attended them.

But, as three individuals, they knew they could only reach so many people. So they developed the Safe Circles website that makes available free workshop materials which anyone can use to educate the children in their community about topics that matter. Resources include presentations, activity sheets and classroom posters. Today, anybody can use the free materials on the Safe Circles website (www.safecircles.lk) to conduct workshops and change the lives of the children in their communities – including you!

Consider conducting an event of your choice in support of a particular cause. Perhaps you could partner with local vets to hold a spay and neuter event for street animals to reduce the number of homeless and unfed animals. Or you could host a workshop, presentation, series of speeches or panel discussion. In order to create an environment that encourages participation and engagement, use segments such as icebreakers, group discussions and interactive activities to encourage participants to share experiences and learn from each other.

In addition, plan how you will evaluate the impact of the event e.g. with participant surveys. This information will be valuable for improving future events you hold.

Conduct a festival

Great if you have skills in: Social intelligence, organising groups, planning and coordination, social media presence

In 1968, the Swedish education minister (and future prime minister) Olof Palme made a speech from the back of a lorry in a park in Sweden. He did so as a tradition for years, and eventually, members of other parliamentary parties began to join him, making the park a vital meeting place for all.

For more than 50 years since, the park has hosted 'democracy festivals' – colourful events to facilitate constructive political dialogue. Today, eight Nordic and Baltic countries, including Denmark, Norway, Sweden and Finland, host democracy festivals.

Free and open to everyone, democracy festivals aim to foster a culture of open discussion, debate and critical thinking among citizens of diverse ages, genders, opinions and backgrounds. They are usually held in the summer and feature food and music, bringing together activists, politicians, entrepreneurs, students and other citizens to sit together and discuss how to make the country a better place to live. Over half a million people take part each year.

In-person events can have a powerful impact on people, so a cause-based festival can be a great way to engage people in a particular cause, create awareness or raise funds. Festivals offer a unique opportunity to bring together people from different backgrounds to celebrate, learn, and take action. You could conduct a festival for people to play with and adopt street animals or a festival focused on women entrepreneurs.

Since a festival is a big undertaking, start by creating a planning team to handle organising, marketing and fundraising. You can work together to determine the scope of the festival, the activities and entertainment that will be offered, such as speakers, workshops, performances, and interactive exhibits, and the resources and funds needed to make it a success. In order to ensure that the festival runs smoothly and is safe for participants, you may need to arrange security, medical staff, and other personnel.

After the planning committee has developed a budget and timeline, start promoting the event using social media, email marketing, flyers, etc. Be sure to connect with organisations that are working towards the same cause. By planning well, you can create a festival that engages and inspires participants to take action and make a difference.

Canadian-born Amanda Rose decided to combine her twin loves – social change and social media – by organising a night out for Twitter users ("tweeps") in London in support of a local non-profit for the homeless. The event raised £1000 and 14 boxes of canned foods. This inspired Amanda to think bigger. She asked dozens of people in her network if they would recruit volunteers to host similar events in their own cities. When she posted the idea on Twitter, over 100 cities signed up within a week.

Soon Twestival Global was launched, a festival to raise money for charity which took place simultaneously in over 200 cities around the world! The entire quarter million dollars raised went towards providing access to water in Ethiopia.

The following year, Twestival Global raised nearly half a million dollars to combat hunger and sickness in 25 countries. The next year, 150 cities took part in Twestival Local, where volunteers conducted festivals in support of local charities in their own countries. Since its inception, Twestival has raised USD 1.8 million for more than 300 non-profits worldwide.

Start a tradition

Great if you have skills in: Social intelligence, planning and coordination, public speaking

Shyam Sunder Paliwal is from the village of Piplantri in India. In Piplantri, as in many parts of the country, daughters were considered to be a financial burden on the family and undervalued in comparison with boys, who were expected to provide financial support to their parents. But when Shyam lost his beloved 17-year-old daughter to dehydration, he was devastated. He decided to plant a tree in her honour. When others in the village followed suit, as the village head, Shyam saw the potential to start a larger programme.

Today, every time a girl is born in Piplantri, the villagers come together to plant 111 trees to honour the new arrival and support the environment. Over 350,000 trees have been planted, covering approximately 1,000 hectares of previously barren land with a variety of species – from mango to sandalwood to neem trees. Parents also pledge to allow their girls to finish school and not to marry them off before they turn 18. The community further contributes towards opening a fixed deposit account for each girl with INR 31,000 (about USD 380) which she can access once she turns 18.

"Earlier they (girls) were considered a burden. Now we don't think that way. We have no particular desire for sons."
Nanubhai Paliwal, Piplantri resident

Simple actions performed regularly can add up. Try engaging a group of people to take part in a regular activity that contributes to a cause. This can occur on a daily, weekly, monthly or annual basis, or can be tied to particular calendar events, seasons, milestones, etc. For example, you can engage a group of friends to donate blood to hospital patients each month or begin a tradition of organising a food drive during a major holiday season.

Give an award

Great if you have skills in: Social intelligence, organising groups, planning and coordination, social media presence

Kat Gordon is the founder of the 3% Movement, an organisation she set up to increase the ratio of female leaders in the advertising industry. One day, she received a call from the team at the Athena Film Festival. They had spent nine years celebrating films featuring women leaders and now felt it was also important to tackle the world's most pervasive media – advertising.

Kat jumped on board and the Athena Advertising Awards was born. The Athena Advertising Awards recognise and celebrate advertising campaigns that challenge stereotypes and promote gender equality. The awards aim to drive positive change in the advertising industry and the world. Previous winners include a group of Polish companies that bought over a Polish porn magazine to put it out of business, with its last ever issue featuring feminist articles and its social media transformed into an educational platform on gender issues.

By recognising deserving people or entities, you highlight the values you want to see flourish in the world. On behalf of your organisation, school or club, consider how you can give an award to an individual or entity whose efforts deserve public recognition. In doing so, you will be shining a spotlight on powerful principles. Speak to the head of the organisation you represent about your idea, and seek out relevant sponsors who can provide funding for the awards event.

"One of the primary goals of the Athena Film Festival is to challenge the way society views and values women. In many ways, those views and values are shaped by advertising."
Kathryn Kolbert, Athena Film Festival co-founder

Resist oppression

Great if you have skills in: Social intelligence, negotiation, public speaking

Pakistan born Malala Yousafzai was an excellent student and loved going to school. But when the terrorist group the Taliban took control of her home area, they started burning down girls' schools. Malala's father took her to a local press club where, at the age of 11, she made a speech in support of girls' right to education. She also worked with BBC Urdu to publish 35 diary entries about what life under Taliban rule was like. In 2009, Malala made a television appearance on a popular Pakistani talk show to stress the importance of girls' education. In the same year, a New York Times reporter worked with her to make a short film called 'Class Dismissed'. With all of Malala's efforts and activism, she drew local and international recognition. This also made her a target of the Taliban.

In 2012, when Malala was 15, while she was returning home from school, a Taliban gunman entered the school bus she was in and asked "Who is Malala?" He shot her on the left side of the head. Malala was flown to England for surgery, where she woke up 10 days later. Following her recovery, she returned to her studies and her activism. On her 16th birthday, Malala spoke at the United Nations. Together with her father, she set up the Malala Fund, a charity devoted to ensuring every girl's right to education and a future of her choice.

Malala received the Nobel Peace Prize in 2014 for her activism, becoming the youngest-ever Nobel laureate.

You too can create social change by defying what oppressors expect from you and continuing to do what you know to be just. This could mean refusing to change seats on a bus like Rosa Parks or continuing to speak out and attend school like Malala Yousafzai. You could also follow the example of Mohandas Gandhi.

When Mohandas was a child growing up in India, he was not exceptional in his studies. A report described him as: "Good at English, fair in Arithmetic and weak in Geography; conduct very good, bad handwriting." Even as he entered adulthood, he was terrified of speaking in public and had no interest in politics. Then, he took a job in South Africa as a young lawyer and found himself faced with racism. He was asked to remove his turban by a court magistrate, thrown out of a train, beaten up, and barred from hotels – all because of the colour of his skin. All these experiences awakened Mohandas' strong sense of equality and justice.

Mohandas introduced the concept of satyagraha ("devotion to truth"), a non-violent form of protest where individuals would defy unjust laws enforced by India's colonial rulers and peacefully suffer the consequences of their defiance. Thousands of Indians were jailed and many even killed for their peaceful resistance, sacrificing their freedom and lives for dignity and self-respect. The British government eventually found that they could not keep up their brutality with the world watching, and ultimately withdrew from India. As the leader of the movement against British rule of India which finally lead to the nation's independence, Mohandas – now respectfully called Mahatma Gandhi – came to be considered the father of his country.

Leverage social media

Great if you have skills in: Social media presence, social intelligence, photography, writing

Australian Rebecca Prince-Ruiz was concerned about the amount of plastic going to landfill and urged her family to go plastic-free for the month of July. She then turned to her colleagues at work: "I'm going plastic-free next month, who wants to join me?" Together they began sharing photos on social media of their efforts to eliminate plastic from their lives. The idea started conversations, spread quickly and ultimately went viral, resulting in the #PlasticFreeJuly social media movement. Since then, over 300 million people around the world have participated in the movement, committing to reduce their plastic use in the month of July, with many inspired to keep it up indefinitely.

Social media is a powerful tool to raise awareness and build momentum. By connecting people across the globe in real-time, it can amplify voices that may have otherwise gone unheard. Movements like the ALS Ice Bucket Challenge, #MeToo and #BlackLivesMatter have grabbed widespread attention and created real change in part because of social media.

Consider using your own social media platforms to start movements, support causes, share informative articles and videos, and connect with others who share your views. As you do so, make a point to also critically analyse what you come across – verify sources, ask questions and seek out alternate viewpoints.

Social media can be especially important as a platform for change if you live in an area where activism is less visible or accepted. By finding and joining groups on social media, you can connect and work together with other passionate changemakers.

CREATIVE IMPACT

"Others have seen what is and asked why.
I have seen what could be and asked why not."
Pablo Picasso

Whether or not you think of yourself as a creative person, you can make something that inspires action, sheds light on complex issues or brings insights into the public consciousness. Unique creations have been used for centuries to amplify important messages, challenge norms and humanise issues. You too can use your power to create to spark change. Let's explore different methods you could use.

Create a video

Great if you have skills in: Filming, video editing, animation, writing, public speaking

When a Unilever thermometer factory in New York faced concerns over mercury poisoning, it moved its operations to the beautiful Indian hill town of Kodaikanal. After dozens of factory workers and children in the area died, the factory had to shut down. High levels of toxic mercury were discovered in the environment around the factory. However, the multinational corporation failed to effectively clean up the contamination or compensate affected families.

In 2015, Indian artist Sofia Ashraf, then 28 years old, called out the company with a powerful rap video showcasing the horrific impacts on the Kodaikanal community and insisting that "Kodaikanal won't step down unless you make amends now". The video, set to the beat of Nicki Minaj's hit song Anaconda (and retweeted by Minaj herself), quickly went viral, garnering over a million views within days. In the face of widespread backlash, Unilever made settlement payments to over 500 of the factory's former workers.

Videos for social causes can have a significant impact in raising awareness and promoting change. They can humanise issues and make them relatable to a wider audience. Videos can also inspire viewers to take action and make a difference.

Consider creating a video to:

- Inform and educate about an issue
- Convey the emotions behind a cause
- Document a marginalised individual's story
- Discuss the history of an issue
- Hold an authority figure accountable

If you're not sure where to start, create a storyboard or script to organise your ideas. Plan to use impactful language and visuals. You could film the video using a smartphone or professional camera, or put your skills in animation to use. Consider using video editing software (including social media tools) to add music, voiceovers and special effects to make your video extra engaging.

Promote the video online with a call to action, perhaps encouraging viewers to sign a petition or donate to a cause. Use platforms such as YouTube and TikTok to further your impact. You can even create a dedicated channel for your cause.

At just six years old, Roman McConn started making and sharing videos in which he introduced and interacted with shelter dogs, and encouraged viewers to adopt them. Roman's cute videos showed viewers how lovable and child-friendly the dogs were, boosting adoption rates. Roman didn't stop there. Alongside his mom, he started Project Freedom Ride which relocates dogs in high-kill zones like Texas to rescue homes or families in Washington. Roman's efforts have saved over 1,300 dogs and Roman was awarded Kid of the Year by the American Society for the Prevention of Cruelty to Animals (ASPCA) in 2018.

Create posters and flyers

Great if you have skills in: Drawing, illustrating, graphic design, digital illustration, writing

In 1942, during World War II, many factories and plants in the United States were struggling to operate as several men had left to fight in the war. Westinghouse Electric Corporation commissioned an artist called J. Howard Miller to create a poster encouraging women to enlist in the workforce. His posters featured 'Rosie the Riveter', a worker in a red bandanna, rolling up her shirt-sleeve and flexing her arm, declaring "We can do it!" The poster became an icon of the feminist movement, encouraging women to take on what were then seen as 'male roles'. Indeed, following a national wartime campaign, an estimated five million women joined the U.S. workforce.

Eye-catching posters and flyers can make an impact, helping to raise awareness, elicit emotion and advocate for a cause. They may be used to provide key information on important issues, promote community events and rallies, and invite viewers to take action.

When designing a poster or flyer, select or create compelling imagery that resonates with your target audience. Develop memorable taglines and slogans, and ensure that your key messages are easy to read and understand. Display or distribute your posters and flyers in high-traffic areas, and consider extending the reach of your message by creating digital versions to share on social media.

Create art

Great if you have skills in: Painting, sculpting, illustrating, drawing, sketching, creating

Shamsia Hassani was born in Tehran, Iran to parents who had escaped Afghanistan due to war. After the fall of the Taliban in 2001, she moved to the capital of Afghanistan, Kabul, to pursue degrees in visual art. Shamsia was determined to paint a new picture of Afghan women for society. As a graffiti artist, she began adorning the walls of Kabul with paintings of bold and independent women, larger than life, full of energy and ready for a fresh start. Some dance and play the piano and the electric guitar.

Shamsia's murals are created in minutes, allowing her to act fast and escape harassment from those who believe that women belonged at home. To reduce the risk of getting caught, she would paint on the narrow streets, passages, alleys and staircases that people used every day, rather than on big buildings. Shamsia's art has inspired women worldwide and given hope to hundreds of Afghan artists, many of whom have showcased their own creativity through Shamsia's university art lessons, graffiti festival, and international exhibitions.

"Graffiti is a friendly way to fight. Most people don't go to art galleries or museums. But if I create my art in the streets, they will see it."
Shamsia Hassani

You can also put your artistic talent to use in favour of your preferred cause(s). For example, by creating a painting, sketch, mural, sculpture, or other piece of art that conveys a socially relevant message. You might create a sketch to encourage vegetarianism, paint a mural that promotes environmental protection, or create a sculpture representing LGBTQIA+ love.

Soon after Ai Weiwei was born, his father, a renowned poet, was exiled by the Chinese government to a remote area for 16 years, along with his family. When Ai was 19, the family returned to the capital city, Beijing. Ai then travelled to New York City to study design, and lived there for 10 years. When his father fell ill, Ai returned to China. He became increasingly critical of the Chinese government. In response, he was beaten, jailed and put under surveillance. Ai managed to leave the country and began creating artwork to protest political oppression in China and around the world. His work includes installations, sculptures, photographs and films.

Several of Ai's artworks draw attention to the plight of refugees. He collected, washed and displayed over 2,000 clothes, shoes and blankets left at a refugee camp. He wrapped the columns of major public institutions in 14,000 life vests used by refugees during perilous journeys. He created a film following hundreds of displaced persons from 23 countries. For one project, Ai used over a million LEGO blocks to create 176 images of political prisoners worldwide. When the LEGO company refused to supply the blocks since they would be used for political reasons, thousands of people donated their own LEGOs in support of his project. Ai continues to use his art to be a voice for political freedom everywhere.

"If my art has nothing to do with people's
pain and sorrow, what is art for?"
Ai Weiwei

Design digital content

Great if you have skills in: Graphic design, digital illustration

When African American George Floyd was killed and the United States was rocked with protests against police brutality, an Irish illustrator called Pan Cooke watched the news unfold from across the sea. He decided to learn more about the issue. As Pan uncovered more and more stories of police brutality and racism, he started creating comics depicting the incidents and sharing them on his Instagram page. He shared the stories of people like Ahmaud Arbery, Breonna Taylor and Eric Garner. The simple, illustrated style of the comics resonated with people and made the heavy subject feel more approachable, while conveying the gravity of the issue. Soon, Pan's following grew rapidly, from under 1,000 to over 300,000 followers. Pan continues to use his platform to spread awareness and invite viewers to support human rights.

"I'm using art to tell a story that's already
available, just in a different way."
Pan Cooke

If you have skills in digital design, or are well versed in using design tools such as Adobe Illustrator or Canva, consider designing creative materials that can inform and educate people about your preferred cause(s). These might take the form of social media posts, infographics, online magazines, presentations, comics, or more. By circulating these widely on social media and through other channels, you can impact the way people think about important issues.

Create a performance

Great if you have skills in: Singing, dancing, writing, acting, public speaking, choreography, organising groups

At 16, Una Torfadóttir of Iceland wrote a three-page slam poem called 'Elsku Stelpur' ('Dear Girls') about what it is like to be a teen girl today. Together with her friends, she created a powerful dance to go along with the poem and emphasise her message about the stranglehold of society on girls. Together, the fiery five-minute spoken word poem and energetic dance create a dramatic interplay that captured national attention.

The performance claimed first place at an Icelandic talent competition and was nationally televised. Every major newspaper and website in the country spoke about the piece. Una and her friend Margrét Snorradóttir, who had started their school's feminist group, were invited to deliver a TEDx talk. Together, they spoke about the topic

'When Girls Take Up Space', inviting the audience to challenge society's limitations. Today, the 'Elsku Stelpur' ('Dear Girls') performance has been viewed over 50,000 times on YouTube.

The performing arts can be powerful way to capture attention. Consider creating and delivering a song, poem, dance or play (or combination of these) to communicate the importance of a cause. You could write a poem about animal rights, create a play to draw attention to discrimination, or choreograph a flash mob to spread a message of kindness.

Introduce a symbol

Great if you have skills in: Graphic design, digital illustration, social media, leadership, organising groups

When pro-democracy protests broke out in Hong Kong in 2014, protesters used yellow umbrellas to shield themselves from tear gas fired by the police. Those yellow umbrellas became a symbol of their fight for democratic rights, and the movement came to be known as the Umbrella Movement.

Symbols can be uniting emblems for movements, ideas and values. They include symbolic colours or objects, flags, the use of lights, sounds, paint, or even hand gestures.

In the *Hunger Games* book and movie series, a three-finger salute was adopted as a symbol of resistance by rebels fighting for freedom against totalitarian rule. In Thailand in 2014, and later in Myanmar, pro-democracy activists used this salute to show their opposition to military rule. Thai authorities were so shaken by the salute that they banned the gesture.

Suffragettes in the early 20th century also used symbolic gestures like raising a hand or pointing a finger to emphasise their demand for the right to vote. These gestures formed part of their visual language of resistance. The suffragettes also used symbolic colors, including white, purple, and gold, in banners, sashes, and flags to represent purity, dignity, and hope.

Consider what symbols would best represent the cause(s) you advocate for. These might be visual symbols, but could even be sounds, such as a unique pattern of clapping or drumming. Besides symbols of protest, you can also create symbols of peace and love, such as the peace sign created by Gerald Holtom or the rainbow flag designed by Gilbert Baker.

Write articles or books

Great if you have skills in: Writing, research, critical analysis

Peter Singer, an Australian moral philosopher, published the book 'The Life You Can Save' in 2009. The book describes how anyone can easily save lives by donating to the people in greatest need via projects that have proven effectiveness in saving lives. The book (and the non-profit he subsequently created with the same name) have helped raise millions of dollars for charity.

In order to help the book reach even more people, and thereby benefit more people living in extreme poverty, Peter bought the rights to the book back from the publisher, and chose to make the book available free of charge in e-book and audiobook formats. Now, anyone can download 'The Life You Can Save' for free at www.thelifeyoucansave.org.

Writing often has the power to make people pay attention or change their perspectives. Consider writing about a cause that you are passionate about. Seek out research from credible sources to augment your words. You can then post your writing on social media, publish it in a blog, circulate it to magazines and newspapers, or compile it into a book.

As an author, this particular change strategy has a special place in my heart. When I wrote my book 'The Utopia Playbook', I was hopeful that it could help more people understand what made certain countries happy and successful. By shining a spotlight on the efforts of nations that lead in happiness, health, inclusivity, and more, I hope to inspire other nations to follow in their footsteps. What would *you* like the world to pay more attention to?

Publish a newsletter or magazine

Great if you have skills in: Writing, research, critical analysis, graphic design, digital illustration, social media, organising groups

Before he turned 30, Graham Hill sold his Internet startup to Microsoft and found himself with more money than he thought he would earn in a lifetime. He bought a four-storey, 3,600-square-foot house in Seattle and filled it with stuff. Yet, he soon found he had to spend loads of time on the upkeep of all his things. When he met and fell in love with a girl from Andorra, he found himself much happier abandoning his things and following her to Barcelona to live in a tiny flat, and then to live out of his backpack with her in different countries around the world. Although the relationship eventually ended, his relationship with material things was changed forever. He now lives in a 420-square-foot studio and is deeply conscious about his carbon footprint.

In 2003, Graham founded TreeHugger, a sustainability website with an e-newsletter that keeps millions of subscribers informed about eco-friendly living, environmental issues, and sustainable practices. The TreeHugger newsletter typically covers topics such as green living tips, conservation efforts, renewable energy, and eco-friendly product recommendations. Its mission is "to take green mainstream", something TreeHugger has been doing for the past 20 years.

Consider starting a newsletter to promote your preferred cause(s). You can focus on stories that may not receive widespread attention, shedding light on underreported issues, and building a community of like-minded individuals. You might want to use your newsletter to encourage your audience to take action, whether through signing petitions, participating in events, or supporting relevant campaigns.

By starting a cause-related newsletter, you can contribute to building a pluralistic and informed society.

Deliver a speech

Great if you have skills in: Writing, public speaking, research

A high school student in Florida, USA, X González was in their school auditorium one day when a former student entered Marjory Stoneman Douglas High School and fatally shot 17 people. A heartbroken X delivered an impassioned speech in front of a federal courthouse to a crowd of hundreds, demanding reform to gun laws so that their high school would be the last one to suffer such a tragedy. Wiping tears from their face with one hand and holding their handwritten speech in the other, X called out politicians for failing to act on behalf of the thousands of lives that had been lost to mass shootings over the previous years.

> *"I wanted people to feel what I was feeling."*
> *X González*

The heartfelt call to action went viral. Video footage of the speech was viewed by millions, and many celebrities shared their comments. The following month, the governor of Florida signed a USD 400 million bill to tighten gun control, including raising the minimum age for purchasing a firearm, introducing mental health support in schools and giving police greater authority to seize weapons. The governor said, "To the students of Marjory Stoneman Douglas High School, you made your voices heard. You didn't let up and you fought until there was change."

Like writing, speeches have the capacity to use powerful language to inform, inspire and persuade. With the added dimension of voice, they can become even more effective. Speeches can take many forms, incorporating poetry, stand-up comedy, etc. Consider who will be in the audience when you are delivering your speech, and tailor your words to create the largest impact with them. Including personal stories and anecdotes will make your speech more relatable, while using powerful metaphors and imagery will help bring your words to life. End your speech with a call to action that is specific, achievable and meaningful.

Martin Luther King Jr. was a pastor in the United States and a member of the executive committee of the National Association for the Advancement of Colored People. Over an 11-year period, he travelled over six million miles and delivered more than 2,500 speeches, speaking out wherever there was injustice. He also wrote several articles and five books. But he is best-known for delivering one speech in particular.

The 'I Have a Dream' address was delivered to an audience of 250,000 people following a peaceful march on Washington D.C. It was delivered at a time when the Civil Rights Act – a piece of legislation to end discrimination based on colour, race, religion or national origin – was being discussed in the United States Congress. A call for equality and freedom, 'I Have a Dream' is often lauded as one of the best and most iconic speeches of all time. Martin Luther King Jr. won the Nobel Peace Prize in 1964 at the age of thirty-five.

"I have a dream that my four little children will one day live in a nation where they will not be judged by the colour of their skin but by the content of their character. I have a dream that, one day, right there in Alabama, little black boys and black girls will be able to join hands with little white boys and white girls as sisters and brothers."
Martin Luther King Jr.

Curate information

Great if you have skills in: Writing, research, graphic design, website or app development

As part of his work, Australian Gordon Renouf would talk to everyday people to find out how to support their rights as consumers. He discovered that they weren't always worried about getting the best prices, but they did want to know whether the items they bought were aligned with their values. Gordon decided to provide that information. Together with some friends, he started Good On You, a website and mobile app that rates over 5,000 fashion brands based on their ethical and environmental practices. An easy-to-understand five-point rating system ('We Avoid', 'Not Good Enough', 'It's a Start', 'Good' and 'Great') now helps over one million people make more sustainable fashion choices and support responsible brands.

"Sustainability is very important to many of us, but it's not the only thing in life. The easier we can make it for you to choose a more sustainable brand over a less sustainable brand that still meets your functional and style needs, the more impact we can have on the world."
Gordon Renouf

By organising information in ways that help others, you can do a lot of good! For example, you could research a cause and present your data simply and persuasively to effect change. You could archive essential information from history, preserving it for the sake of collective memory. Curating information could even be as simple as creating informational pamphlets for people suffering from grief, or posting flyers on recognising and escaping domestic abuse where vulnerable people might see them.

Sometimes, the most valuable way to make a difference might be to draw attention to the entities and resources that already exist. Ask yourself whether the gap in the community is actually a lack of awareness about the supportive avenues that are already out there and how they can help. Consider the case of Aidbox, an app that provides refugees with information on medical, legal, and educational resources in their host countries.

Here are more examples of curating information:

- Identify locations that offer free Wi-Fi and provide the list to underserved schools and shelters
- Compile a list of supportive resources for women in need and give printed flyers to institutions, shelters and police stations
- Create a free resource kit for non-profits to help them access free images, design tools, website hosting, etc. to use in their campaigns
- Compile a list of resource people for journalists to contact on topics of importance such as LGBTQIA+ issues, gender-based violence, etc.
- Post flyers with information on bullying and other youth issues in places where youth will see them

Simply by making the right information available at the right time, you can change the world.

Build an app or website

Great if you have skills in: Website or app development, digital design

When Jay'Aina Patton was a little girl and her father was in prison, she found that talking to him was expensive and challenging – visits and calls cost a lot and envelopes and stamps weren't always available. Her father too felt the pain of not being able to connect with his daughter. After his release, he started a non-profit to help children whose parents are incarcerated send them photos and letters for free.

Jay'Aina, at the age of 10, had been watching over his shoulder as he coded on the computer. She quickly learnt the skill for herself. When she was 12 years old, she saw that her father's initiative needed a mobile app, so she built one within three months. Today, the Photo

Patch app has been used to send over a million photographs and letters, connecting family members. Jay'Aina now helps teach thousands of black students to code as a youth coding instructor at Unlock Academy. Her goal is to personally bring 10,000 women of colour into the tech world.

Consider building an app or a website to support a cause you care about. For example, you might choose to build a tool that equips people in meeting their educational goals or one that supports the needs of a vulnerable group such as people suffering from depression or people with disabilities.

Hans Jørgen Wiberg from Denmark did just that. He was born with the usual span of vision but, over time, the breadth of his vision began to reduce until it covered a mere 5 degrees. Hans found himself having to rely on his neighbour to help him with tasks like distinguishing between the cans in his kitchen cupboard. In speaking with others with visual impairments, he found that they too experienced a few moments a day when they valued support from a sighted person.

When a blind friend told him that they place video calls to friends and family members, Hans got the idea for the 'Be My Eyes' mobile app. This app would connect blind people to a network of sighted volunteers for live video support when needed. He presented the idea at a Danish startup event, and a team volunteered to build the app. Within 24 hours of the app's release, it had over 10,000 users. Today, the app has over 6.5 million sighted volunteers supporting over half a million blind and low-vision users from over 150 countries in more than 180 languages. The app gives individuals with visual impairments the confidence to navigate a variety of environments, knowing that they have a huge community ready to be their eyes at any moment.

Design a new system

Great if you have skills in: Critical analysis, empathy, research

Maria Montessori was one of Italy's first female doctors and well-known for the sincere care she gave her patients. After working with children with mental disabilities, she came to believe that a lack of sensory stimulation in the empty, bare rooms where the kids stayed was worsening their conditions. At the age of 29, she gave a talk at the National Pedagogical Congress describing her vision for social progress based on education.

When Maria was 37, she set up the first 'Casa dei Bambini' or 'Children's House'. She filled the space with materials and activities, then kept only those that she saw engaged the children. She discovered that, provided with instruments and activities that supported their natural development, children could learn by themselves. A year later, five more Children's Houses were set up. The children's progress was so impressive that people flocked to the schools to see for themselves how they operated. Soon, kindergartens across Italy were being transformed into Children's Houses.

Maria's method treated children as individuals, recognising their creative potential and drive to learn. Soon, her book 'The Montessori Method' was published and translated into 20 different languages. Societies, training programmes and schools based on the Montessori method emerged all over the world, and to date, Maria's work has had an enormous impact on childhood education worldwide.

"What really makes a teacher is love for the human child; for it is love that transforms the social duty of the educator into the higher consciousness of a mission."
Maria Montessori

Look around you and observe the systems and processes that are part of the way you and others around you live. Consider, for example, the experiences of children in the foster care system or animals at animal shelters. How could these experiences be improved or transformed? Can you use your imagination and skills to dream up a better way?

Perhaps you can improve on an old process by reimagining and reinventing it. Consider the work of Louis Braille. When Louis was three years old and playing with tools in his father's shop, he was blinded in his right eye, eventually becoming totally blind. He ended up studying at the National Institute for Blind Youth in Paris. One day, the institute was visited by Charles Barbier of Napolean's army. Charles had created a system of note-taking that included embossed dots which represented sounds. This allowed notes to be quietly passed among the army ranks to communicate in the dark, without alerting the enemy. The army was unimpressed, so Charles took his idea to the school for the blind.

Louis was instantly inspired and spent three years improving on the concept. At the age of 15, he came up with a writing system which used six raised dots to spell out various words. In his short life, he adapted the system to be used in music and translated important books. The 'Braille' system he invented is still used in almost every country in the world, improving the lives of millions of people.

Transform a space

Great if you have skills in: Critical analysis, empathy, design

When Doug Dietz saw a little girl crying while being led to the MRI (magnetic resonance imaging) machine he had spent two and a half years designing, it came as a shock. He suddenly realised that the high-tech hospital equipment that he was so proud of represented a terrifying experience for young patients in need of scans. He soon came to know that up to 80% of children in need of MRI scans had to be sedated as they were so frightened that they could not lie still until the scan was complete. Doug was determined to do better.

After undertaking a design thinking workshop at Stanford, he came up with a creative solution. Without changing the machine's technology, he simply used paint and colourful stickers to transform the room and scanner into a colourful adventure scene such as a pirate ship, submarine or rocket ship. Machine operators were then briefed to inform the child about their mission – for example, that they will be taking a sea voyage and to lie still in the ship so they can collect some treasure from the pirate's chest afterwards. The simple solution saw patient satisfaction rise by 90%. The most joyful moment for Doug was hearing a little girl who had just been scanned in the machine say, "Mommy, can we come back tomorrow?"

Can you think of a way to make a space more comfortable, beautiful or inviting, particularly for vulnerable groups? By transforming a space, you can transform someone's experience for the better, especially during a time of stress or discomfort.

When Temple Grandin was three and a half, she was diagnosed with autism. Rejecting advice to put her in an institution, Temple's parents instead sent her to private schools, nurturing her intelligence. While Temple was in high school, she created a 'squeeze machine' designed to give comfort to her autistic body, which is hyper-sensitive to sound and touch.

Temple recognised that animals being processed at slaughter houses also experienced intense fear connected with hyper-sensitivity. Armed with degrees in psychology and animal science, she shaped her career around designing more humane livestock processing facilities that minimised the fear and pain experienced by animals. Temple was appointed professor of Animal Science at Colorado State University, and today, half the cattle in the United States are handled in facilities she has designed.

SOCIAL ENTREPRENEURSHIP

"Please think about your legacy,
because you're writing it every day."
Gary Vaynerchuck

Social entrepreneurship is rooted in the belief that business can be a force for good in society. Creating a business with a social aim can be a powerful way to make a difference. Being able to earn while doing good can empower you with the resources to spend more time and effort on your preferred cause(s). It also allows you to reinvest profits back into the business of creating positive change, thereby accelerating your impact. Here are some ideas for different types of social businesses you could start.

Provide a service

Great if you have skills in: Strategic planning, organising groups, leadership, specific technical skills

Food waste is a persistent problem. Did you know that, in 2019, 35% of the food supply in the United States went unsold or uneaten? In 2011, when Ben Simon was a student at the University of Maryland in the United States, he and three friends started the Food Recovery Network. Its aim was to save dining hall food that would otherwise go to waste. In its first four years, Food Recovery Network became the largest student movement against hunger, with chapters in more than 150 colleges.

Wanting to do more to fight food waste, Ben started Imperfect Foods in 2015. First, he would buy the fruits and vegetables that large retailers would not buy from farmers due to cosmetic blemishes (such as the produce being too big, too small or unusually shaped) or because of excess stock. After buying the produce at discounted rates, Ben would sell them directly to consumers through an online subscription service. Subscribers would pick out what they wanted each week and have the food delivered to their doorsteps. The chance to grab nutritious food at discounted rates while benefitting the environment and the farming community was a no-brainer for customers. It's no wonder Imperfect Foods now has over 400,000 customers and 1,500 employees across 38 states in the USA, and has saved over 160 million pounds of food.

As you can see, one way of making a difference while making a living is by offering a service that helps improve the world. For example, you could provide a grocery shopping service for elderly community members, offer low-cost graphic design and online marketing for non-profits, or provide corporations with training programmes on gender sensitivity in the workplace. Consider how you can put your skills to use in providing something that could transform your community and beyond.

Sell a physical product

Great if you have skills in: Strategic planning, organising groups, leadership, specific technical skills

31-year-old Jasmine Taylor was dramatically in debt, with about USD 70,000 in student loans, medical and credit card debt. In an effort to get better at managing her money, she started practicing a budgeting approach that she had learnt about on YouTube. The technique, referred to as 'cash stuffing', involved pre-determining how much would be spent on each category of expenses every month, and placing that amount in cash in labelled envelopes. Once the envelopes are empty, spending stops. By making the budgeting process more concrete, visible and physical, cash stuffing empowers individuals who struggle with money management to get control over their finances. Jasmine began sharing videos of her process on TikTok to hold herself accountable, and became increasingly popular. She now has over 800,000 followers.

Jasmine decided to begin offering products to help others take control of their finances in the same way that she did. She put her savings towards starting an e-commerce business, selling attractively designed wallets with cute pictures and slogans and categorised envelopes. Buyers are able to customise the envelopes with their choice of design and expense categories – thus making saving cute and fun. Today, Jasmine's business Baddies & Budgets is on track to bring in USD 1 million.

You too could provide a product that offers a social or environmental benefit. Your product does not need to be a brand-new invention. It could simply be a socially or environmentally conscious alternative to an existing product. For example, you might choose to sell reusable period products to replace disposable ones, provide makeup to suit a more diverse range of skin tones, or sell ethically sourced clothing.

Offer a digital product

Great if you have skills in: Website and app development, digital design, marketing

While dining at a buffet restaurant in Denmark, 22-year-old Thomas Momsen wondered how much food at the location would end up being thrown away. He told his friends Stian Olesen and Klaus Pedersen his idea for a tool that would help to redistribute excess food at grocery stores, restaurants and bakeries to hungry individuals at one-third the retail price. The three decided to make it a reality.

They set up a simple website and called buffet restaurants to encourage them to sign up by indicating when they would make food available for sale and when customers could pick it up. Within two months, Too Good to Go had 100 participating restaurants and had become known across Denmark. This was followed by a rigorous global expansion. Today, the company has expanded to over 15 countries and has more than 75 million users. It has saved over 200 million meals across the world by partnering with more than 130,000 retailers.

By creating a digital product such as an app or online course that supports a cause, entrepreneurs can transform the lives of others while making a living.

Ways in which to earn from a digital cause-based product might include by taking a small commission from every transaction your app or website facilitates, generating ad revenue by displaying advertisements alongside valuable information, or by directly selling a cause-based digital product such as a meaningful online course.

Provide employment

Great if you have skills in: Organising groups, leadership

South African Tracey Chambers was an accountant at a large department store, Woolworths. After 15 years at the company, despite advancing in her corporate career, she didn't feel a sense of satisfaction. At the age of 40, she quit her job without a clear idea of what she wanted to do next. The following year, while in conversation with a friend, she made an insightful connection. She remembered how Woolworths used to struggle to manage its excess clothing stock, and also recalled how the lady who helped her with housework had made a good income by reselling Tracey's second-hand clothes.

Tracey teamed up with her old friend Tracey Gilmore to start The Clothing Bank. They invited major clothing retailers to donate their excess stock, damaged and returned items, saving them from being burnt or sent to landfill. At The Clothing Bank, the items are sold to unemployed South African mothers at deep discounts, and the women resell the items. In a nation with the highest rates of unemployment in the world, the model provides women with financial independence while helping the environment. In 2019, retailers donated over 1.8 million units, valued at cost at USD 8 million. This generated collective profits of about USD 2.4 million for 900 women business owners. Tracey has since introduced a unit for unemployed South African fathers to repair and resell appliances.

As a social entrepreneur, you could provide employment and earnings to people from marginalised or vulnerable communities by engaging their efforts in creating a product or providing a service. For example, you might employ deaf individuals in providing foot massages or sell products made by people from households struck by poverty.

That's what Nana Frimpong Abebrese did. A charismatic farmer from Ghana, he wanted to support cocoa farmers in selling their own cocoa, and secured the help of a fairtrade company to launch a chocolate co-operative – a legal entity that would be owned by the farmers. More than 2,000 farmers took part, and the co-operative was called Kaupa Kokoo ('good cocoa farmer' in the local Twi language) with the motto 'Pa pa paa' ('the best of the best'). Ownership by farmers was a priority, as was paying farmers fair prices in cash, and reinvesting profits back into the community.

Kaupa Kokoo's 'Divine' chocolate bar was introduced to UK supermarket shelves in 2002. Due to its delicious taste and inspiring social mission, the chocolate quickly became popular. Within years, the company had expanded to the USA and Sweden. Today, the farmers own the biggest portion of the company. Over 100,000 Ghanian farmers continue to benefit from a guaranteed minimum price for their cocoa, a fairtrade premium of USD 240 per tonne of cocoa (this is reinvested in the community), a portion of the annual turnover of the company, plus over 40% of the distributed profit.

Invent a product

Great if you have skills in: Research, critical analysis, science, technology, design

When Kavita Shukla was 12 years old and visiting her grandmother in India, she accidentally swallowed tap water while brushing her teeth. Her grandmother quickly served her a homemade concoction that contained ground fenugreek seeds, and assured her she would be alright. Despite her scepticism, Kavita drank the murky brown drink and found she didn't fall sick.

On returning home to the United States, Kavita started experimenting with fenugreek, studying its antifungal and antibacterial properties. She discovered that food wrapped in fenugreek-treated paper could last four to six weeks longer than was typical. What was more, the paper was biodegradable, non-toxic, and could be produced easily in large quantities. At the age of 17, Kavita patented FreshPaper. She started handing it out at farmers' markets, and soon the product was in demand.

After graduating from Harvard, Kavita started Fenugreen, a company which today sells FreshPaper in more than 35 countries. Fenugreen is even partnering with non-governmental organisations to provide access to FreshPaper to support the 1.6 billion people in the world who don't have refrigeration facilities.

"It's a very simple kind of concept, and I think that was almost what held me back for a long time because I kept thinking, you know, it's so simple. But then I realised that's really what made it so special."
Kavita Shukla

Look around and consider what might make the world a better place, and how you might use your skills to make it a reality. You may be able to invent a brand-new product with world-changing potential!

That's exactly what Boyan Slat from Netherlands did. When he was 16 years old and scuba diving on vacation, he was shocked that he could see more plastic bags than fish in the ocean. He wondered, "Why can't we just clean this up?" He began exploring ways to use technology to clean up the ocean. He eventually invented multiple technologies to clean up the ocean as well as stop plastic waste in rivers from ever reaching the sea.

Boyan's invention 'The Interceptor' intercepts plastic in major rivers before it reaches the ocean. Today, there are interceptors placed in the world's most heavily polluting rivers. His technology is also actively cleaning up an area of the Pacific Ocean known as the Great Pacific Garbage Patch. Through his organisation, The Ocean Cleanup, Boyan wants to remove 90% of floating ocean plastic by 2040 – and he seems to be well on his way to making it happen!

Donate with every sale

Great if you have skills in: Strategic planning, budgeting

When Blake Mycoskie visited Argentina in 2006 at the age of 29, he was saddened to see the challenges faced by little children without shoes. Some suffered from blisters and infections, others could not attend school. He met a lady who was helping with a shoe donation drive, but learnt from her that dependence on donations made it difficult to consistently supply shoes. Yet, the impact the shoes had on the local community made an impression on him. He watched a mother weep when her sons – who had been sharing one pair of adult-sized shoes and taking turns going to school – each received shoes that fit their own feet.

Blake decided that he would start a special kind of shoe company. For every pair of shoes sold, the company would donate a pair to a child in need. He called the company Shoes for Tomorrow, later shortened to Tomorrow's Shoes, then to TOMS. TOMS' social mission and inspiring one-for-one business model turned the company into a movement. Within seven years, TOMS had donated over 10 million shoes to children around the world.

Making donations to correspond with your sales can help turn any company into a social business. For example, each time you make a sale or cross a sales threshold, you could donate products to communities in need of them, provide free services to worthy recipients, or donate a percentage of your profits to a relevant cause. That last one is what Yvon Chouinard does.

Yvon Chouinard, now in his 80s, was an avid rock-climber in his youth. At one time, he lived out of his car and would buy damaged cans of cat food for 5 cents each to eat. But Yvon had a pioneering spirit. He founded the Patagonia clothing and outdoor gear company. Patagonia was one of the first companies to prioritise environmental sustainability in its supply chain and products.

An active environmentalist, Yvon founded '1% for the Planet' and Patagonia became the first company to pledge 1% of its yearly sales to the environment. More than USD 140 million has been donated as a result of Yvon's pledge. In 2022, Yvon and his family generously transferred their ownership of Patagonia, worth about USD 3 billion, to a specially designed trust. This trust will ensure that *all* of Patagonia's profits (about USD 100 million a year) will go towards combatting climate change.

"Now I could die tomorrow and the company
is going to continue doing the right thing for the
next 50 years, and I don't have to be around."
Yvon Chouinard

A GIVING LIFESTYLE

"What good shall I do today?"
Benjamin Franklin

Every person on the planet can contribute to make the world a better place. The world is full of problems in need of solutions, and there is always something any person can do to help make the world better. If you have time or resources at hand, consider using them to make a difference. Here are a few ideas on how to do so.

Be an example

Great if you have skills in: Empathy, social intelligence

Since 2013, when she was 20, singer Ariana Grande has been vegan due to her love of animals. One year after making the change, she updated her over 10 million Twitter fans that it was the happiest, healthiest, and most life-changing decision she had ever made. Ariana also has 10 dogs (and one pig) that live with her, the majority of which are rescues. In 2020, she went a step further and co-founded an animal rescue non-profit to give more animals loving homes.

"I love animals more than I love most people, not kidding!"
Ariana Grande

One of the simplest ways to make a difference is by being an example of someone who lives in an ethical manner. For example, by going vegan, refusing to use disposable products or supporting socially responsible businesses. Simply being the person who says "I don't need a bag" when offered a plastic one at the grocery store might encourage another person watching to rethink their own behaviour. If you are a parent, you inevitably have an audience that is constantly watching and absorbing your example.

You can also gear up to do good. For example, by keeping spare change, a first aid kit or jumper cables handy for anyone in need, packing an extra meal for a homeless person, or learning CPR so you are ready to help if the need arises.

Remember, you can't force anyone else to make changes in their own lives, but you can inspire them through your behaviour. Often, your best bet for promoting ethical practices and creating positive change is to be a living example.

When Lauren Singer was a 21-year-old studying environmental studies, she looked in her fridge and realised how many items were packaged in plastic. She decided in that moment to quit plastic. While doing her research online, she came across a lady called Bea Johnson who ran a zero-waste home, and was deeply inspired. She began taking her own bags and jars to the store and shopping at farmers' markets to get her produce package-free. Next, she started making her own products such as toothpaste, lotion and deodorant so she wouldn't need to buy anything packaged in plastic. Lauren also started buying recycled clothes second-hand so she wouldn't be putting new waste into the waste cycle. She cut down on the items she owned and began composting. Along the way, she documented her journey on her blog 'Trash is for Tossers'. Three years later, all the waste that she had produced could fit into a single jar.

The image of Lauren's jar provided a concrete picture of what a plastic-free life could look like. Today, Lauren's TEDx talk about her lifestyle has been viewed more than 4.5 million times, and her blog inspires millions of people around the world to produce less waste.

Be present

Great if you have skills in: Empathy, social intelligence

When Agnes Gonxha Bojaxhiu was 18 years old, she left her family home to become a nun. After training in Ireland, she was sent to India, and this was where she took her vows as a nun and adopted the name Teresa. For 17 years, she taught at a Calcutta high school, but the suffering that she saw around her led her to ask for permission to leave the school and work among the destitute people in the slums. She began an open-air school for impoverished children, and although she did not have funds, she was soon supported by volunteers and donors.

Within two years, she had started her own order 'The Missionaries of Charity'. Its aim was to love and look after the people that nobody else was willing to care for. Her order set up centres to serve people who were terminally ill, blind, elderly and disabled. She was awarded the Nobel Peace Prize in 1979. At the time of her death, she left behind a legacy of hundreds of centres across over 90 countries staffed with about 4,000 nuns and hundreds of thousands of people. Today, Mother Teresa is a global symbol of peace and love.

Research shows that volunteering brings a host of benefits to volunteers – 78% of volunteers say it lowers stress levels, 94% say it improves their mood, 96% say it enriches their sense of purpose. Whether it's working with a local charity, answering helpline calls, volunteering with a meaningful political campaign, or helping out at a community centre, there are endless opportunities to make a difference by giving your time.

Your presence alone can be of great comfort to someone else, easing their loneliness and helping them to feel seen and valued. Consider volunteering at an elders' home, children's orphanage, or a care facility for hospice patients or persons with disabilities. You can read to the residents, play boardgames, sing songs, dance, teach crafts, or simply chat about each of your life experiences. Even within your own circle of family, friends and acquaintances, you may know someone who would deeply value a letter, visit, or friend, so consider sharing your time with them.

Animal shelters also often need volunteers to assist in feeding the animals, walking dogs, cleaning shelters and helping to rehabilitate traumatised animals. If animals make your heart light up, consider giving your time to them.

If you are passionate about the environment, you could volunteer to plant flowers and trees in public spaces, paint public walls, pick up rubbish and clean beaches. Or simply take a bag with you to collect trash on your route whenever you go out for a walk. Those who see you do so might start to do the same!

Volunteer skills

Great if you have skills in: Social intelligence, teaching, specific technical skills

In 2004, 27-year-old Sal Khan heard from his aunt that his cousin Nadia was struggling with unit conversion in her mathematics curriculum. Sal made a deal with Nadia that he would spend an hour after work remotely tutoring her, provided she would do the extra work he set for her. She agreed. They would talk over the telephone and use Yahoo Doodle as a shared virtual notepad. Nadia quickly caught up, word spread, and more and more family members wanted Sal's tutoring. When scheduling became complicated, he decided to make videos and post them on YouTube so his family members could learn at their own pace. On YouTube, the videos were accessible to anyone.

Soon, he was receiving letters from students worldwide appreciating his guidance and the engaging way it was delivered. Moved by the impact he was making, he decided to make teaching the focus of his life. He started Khan Academy, a non-profit organisation providing free, world-class online education to anyone, anywhere, regardless of their background or circumstances.

Khan Academy is today available as an online web platform with over 145 million registered users. It features thousands of 10- to 20-minute videos that anyone can learn from, free of charge, and is available in more than 50 languages, with exercises, growth paths and detailed data crunching built in. Many young people credit Khan Academy with transforming their educational lives and careers. In 2012, Sal was recognised as one of TIME magazine's "100 Most Influential People in the World". Sal's work has also encouraged other socially-minded creators. Andrew Ng, who founded Coursera, one of the world's first massive open online course platforms, says that Sal was a huge inspiration.

Like Sal, consider using your skills to help others. There are many ways you can do this. You could volunteer to take photos for a charity event, teach meditation in schools or prisons, help someone with their resumé, get a charity set up on social media, build a website for a non-profit, or teach vocational skills like technology and languages. The list is endless!

Teaching, training and mentoring are great ways to help. Look for opportunities to volunteer your time and talent at local clubs, organisations and libraries. You could conduct an after-school programme at a local school, teach someone with learning difficulties to read, or offer youth swimming lessons. If you know multiple languages (including sign language), you can also offer to translate, dub or provide interpretations for valuable content so that it's available to more people.

If you're a professional, you can share your professional abilities with others. For example, lawyers can provide pro-bono legal services to those in need, doctors can volunteer their time to provide medical care to underserved communities, and accountants can help non-profit organisations with their finances.

Since 2020, I have lent my basic technical skills towards helping secluded seniors connect with their college batchmates around the world via Zoom to celebrate birthdays and other occasions. Seeing how enthusiastically they celebrate with lively chatter, songs, instruments and even magic shows always brightens my day. In fact, the same group made me tear up by surprising me with my own online birthday party complete with poems, paintings and live music!

Be a donor

Great if you have skills in: Empathy

The kidney is the only organ that can be donated by a living donor, since there are two of them. Yet, every day in the United States, 17 people die waiting for a kidney donation. When Alexander Berger learnt that kidney donation in the United States is extremely safe, at 21 years old, he decided to donate one of his kidneys to a stranger. Alexander felt that the chance to give another person an average of 10 more years of life they would not have had otherwise was an opportunity he could not pass up.

Apart from helping the person who received his kidney – a ninth-grade math teacher with two young sons – Alexander ended up benefitting six lives by starting a kidney donation chain. This occurs when a person unable to donate a kidney to their loved one as they are not a match instead donates that kidney to another person in need who has a friend or relative whose kidney is a match for their loved one. As a result, both individuals in need have access to a matching kidney donor. In this way, a chain of donations can benefit many recipients. Alexander has also inspired other individuals who heard about his generosity to make similar donations.

"I feel like it was totally the right decision;
I am really glad I made it and I would do it again."
Alexander Berger

By being a donor, you can save lives. One blood donation can potentially save up to three lives, and one deceased organ donor can save up to eight lives. A kidney donor can give another person 10-20 years of additional life. Meanwhile, one tissue donor (who gives skin tissue, bone tissue or corneas) can benefit the lives of as many as 75 people.

You can sign up to donate your organs (like your heart, lungs and eyes) and tissues after you die, or even donate one of your kidneys as a living donor. You could also regularly donate blood to hospitals or join a bone marrow registry. You can even donate hair to be made into wigs for children with alopecia or cancer. And you can also encourage others to become donors too, thus expanding the circle of giving!

Activate others

Great if you have skills in: Social intelligence, social media presence, organising groups, public speaking, teaching

After graduating from the University of Oxford in the United Kingdom, Benjamin Todd was curious about what to do with his life. One thing he knew was that he wanted to make a positive difference in the world. Yet, he couldn't find the resources to help him make a fulfilling career choice that would have the biggest possible social impact. He and his friend William MacAskill started doing the research themselves. They presented their early ideas in a lecture and were surprised to find that many in the audience decided to change their careers as a result!

Benjamin and William decided to start an organisation devoted to studying the question of how to have a fulfilling career with the biggest possible impact. Named '80,000 Hours' after the approximate amount of time a person will spend on their career over a lifetime, the organisation provides a free career guide (80000hours.org) with serious research into the relative impact different careers could have. It now also offers a podcast, job board, book, and one-on-one guidance, and has reached over 10 million people. In fact, over 1,000 people have said they have changed their careers to have a greater social impact as a result of engaging with 80,000 Hours.

As you can see, one way to make a big difference is to help *others* to do so. If you can provide other people with the information, tools, connections, structure and resources they need to have a big positive impact, you can potentially multiply your own impact. Whether you are organising a group of volunteers to work on a cause, inspiring people to make donations, or training individuals in sign language, by making superheroes out of others, you are building a justice league for the world!

David Nott also sought to shepherd the next generation of changemakers. When David's father, an orthopaedic surgeon with Indian heritage, took him to see the 1984 film *The Killing Fields*, David decided that helping people in desperate situations was how he wanted to spend his life. He went on to become a surgeon who would volunteer to work in dangerous war zones, earning the nickname of the 'Indiana Jones of surgery' by risking his life to provide medical aid in high-conflict areas. David takes up to six weeks of unpaid leave every year to volunteer in places like Afghanistan, Gaza, Iraq, Sierra Leone, Syria and Ukraine.

While on a mission in Libya, David realised that local medical staff at the frontlines did not have the training they needed to deal with the kinds of injuries they were facing. Alongside his wife, he set up a foundation to provide local healthcare workers in disaster and war zones with training in emergency surgery, and the capacity to train others too. The foundation's vision is to create a global network of medical professionals ready to provide the best possible care to patients in war and disaster zones. The David Nott Foundation has now trained over a thousand doctors across 17 countries.

> *"To be able to help people who really needed it, who wouldn't otherwise have help, was something fantastic"*
> *David Nott*

Get a high-impact job

Great if you have skills in: Social intelligence, negotiation, specific technical skills

Simran Dhaliwal was working as a research analyst at the renowned investment banking company Goldman Sachs. She was even recognised as one of the best sell-side stockpickers in London. Yet, she yearned to apply her skills towards a job that could benefit humanity as she had always been struck by the injustice she saw in the world.

In 2019, Simran took the plunge and joined Longview Philanthropy as its Managing Director. Longview Philanthropy encourages wealthy individuals like top YouTubers, bestselling authors and major philanthropists to make philanthropic donations that benefit the future of humanity. Within the first year of her joining, Simran was impressed by how successful the organisation was, and felt incredibly excited and motivated to work in an area that she truly cared about. She now coordinates the organisation's research, grantmaking and advocacy work as its Co-CEO.

Every individual spends a huge portion of time on their careers. By devoting that period of time to a career that can have a positive impact on the world, you can maximise your individual contribution. When selecting what it is you want to do with your life (or rethinking what you are currently doing), consider choosing a career that would benefit society.

Benjamin Todd and William MacAskill's website, 80000hours.org, is devoted to helping individuals find high-impact jobs that suit their interests, skills and capabilities. It makes the case that your choice of career represents your biggest opportunity to make a difference. Consider visiting the website and exploring ways to change the world through your work.

Be a role model

Great if you have skills in: Social intelligence, social media presence

As an Indigenous Australian, Cathy Freeman was well aware of the plight faced by Aboriginal people. Her own grandmother had been forcibly taken away from her family at just eight years old. Yet the government refused to apologise for such injustices, leading over a quarter million Australians to march over the Sydney Harbour Bridge in protest.

For a long time, Aboriginal Australians had been treated as inferior. But Cathy knew she was not. She loved running from the time she was a little girl, and as a teenager, she dreamed of winning an Olympic gold medal. At the age of 16, Cathy won gold in the 400-metre race at the Commonwealth Games. And when the Olympics came to Sydney, she claimed the Olympic gold medal. When doing her victory lap in front of 112,000 ecstatic people, she carried both the Australian and Aboriginal flags, tying their ends together to demonstrate their equal importance to her. The act defied Olympic protocol, which only allowed national flags. But Cathy was unstoppable, and by the following year, the Indigenous flag had been recognised as an official flag of Australia.

"No one was going to stop me telling the world how proud I was to be Aboriginal. I wanted to shout, 'Look at me, look at my skin! I'm black and I'm the best!'"
Cathy Freeman

By being a top performer in a visible field, you can make an impact. You can become a role model and a source of inspiration to those who share your nationality, race, gender, socioeconomic background, etc. In showing the world your capabilities, you can help break down stereotypes and inspire others to follow in your footsteps. So stand up and stand out!

Be a politician

Great if you have skills in: Social intelligence, public speaking, negotiation, debate, leadership

In 2019, Sanna Marin became the world's youngest serving state leader at the age of 34. Sanna, the child of a poor family who was the first in her family to go to university, was a member of parliament in Finland since 2015. YouTube video clips of her effectively chairing sometimes argumentative city council meetings had a large role to play in securing the public's confidence in her.

Sanna's female-majority government enjoyed some of Finland's highest approval ratings – over 70% in 2020. Her agenda was focused on protecting social equality in Finland and addressing climate change. She also responded briskly and decisively to the COVID-19 pandemic, saving citizens' lives. And for all five years that Sanna was prime minister, Finland was named the happiest country in the world by the World Happiness Index!

"I want to build a society where every child can become anything and every person can live and grow in dignity."
Sanna Marin

Politicians hold responsibility for making policies and laws that can impact the lives of millions of people, shaping society and determining the direction of a nation.

While politics is often viewed negatively due to the media attention on scandals and corruption, there are many reasons to consider becoming a politician. Politics can be a challenging and demanding career, requiring long hours and significant sacrifice, and involving criticism and scrutiny from the media and the public. But for those who are passionate about creating positive change, a career in politics can be incredibly rewarding and fulfilling. By working to address issues such as poverty, healthcare and education, politicians can help ensure the country is headed towards a better future.

Politics also provides a platform for individuals to voice their opinions and advocate for change. Politicians can raise awareness on important issues and bring attention to causes that may otherwise go unnoticed. By becoming a politician, you can use your voice to fight for important issues and improve society.

Do medical research

Great if you have skills in: Medicine and biology, research

When Jack Andraka was 13 years old, he lost a dear family friend to pancreatic cancer. Jack came to learn that over 85% of pancreatic cancers are diagnosed late, resulting in patients having a mere 2% survival rate. So the teenager went online looking for answers. He found a database of 8,000 different proteins found in those who have pancreatic cancer. He decided to study each of these proteins and identify which one could provide an indicator for an improved pancreatic cancer test. On the 4,000th try, he found it – a protein called mesothelin which shows up in high levels in the blood when a person has pancreatic, ovarian or lung cancer, even at the earliest stages.

While secretly reading an article about carbon nanotubes in his high school biology class, he saw an opportunity to combine carbon nanotubes with what the teacher was talking about that day – antibodies – to create an effective test for mesothelin.

Jack then sent emails to 200 professors who had touched on pancreatic cancer at Johns Hopkins University and the National Institutes of Health. He received 199 rejection letters. But one professor was willing to give him a chance. After surviving an interrogation of his idea by 20 PhDs, he finally secured the lab space he needed. Yet, he quickly found that his concept had unexpected holes. Over the course of seven months, he plugged those holes one by one until, at the age of 15, he had developed a simple paper sensor that was 168 times faster (taking just 5 minutes to run), over 26,000 times less expensive (costing just 3 cents) and over 400 times more sensitive than the existing pancreatic cancer test. Jack's invention earned him numerous awards and recognition and, more importantly, has the potential to save countless lives.

Medical research can lead to new treatments and therapies for diseases and conditions that were previously untreatable or poorly understood. And research on public health issues like tobacco use, obesity, and air pollution can help policymakers make smart decisions about how to correct these issues at a population level. If you are interested in the medical space, consider using your time and knowledge to save and improve lives.

Consider the work of Jonas Salk. When Jonas was an assistant professor of epidemiology (the study of diseases) at the University of Michigan, he reconnected with an old friend and mentor who taught him how to develop vaccines. A few years later, Jonas started to research an infectious virus that was affecting hundreds of thousands of children. It was called polio. This frightening disease could result in permanent paralysis of the limb, throat or chest muscles.

Jonas believed that injecting 'killed' strains of the polio virus into a person could, without infecting the person, cause their body to produce antibodies to fight the virus. This would effectively make the person immune to the disease. He tested his vaccine on himself and other volunteers, including his wife and children. Soon, as the vaccine proved safe and effective, a national rollout began and the number of polio cases dropped from over 45,000 a year to less than 1,000.

Jonas never patented his vaccine nor made any money from it, preferring instead that it was accessible to as many as possible.

"Who owns the patent on this vaccine?
Well, the people, I would say."
Jonas Salk

Make an investment

Great if you have skills in: Budgeting, finance

When Matt Flannery, Jessica Jackley, Premal Shah and Chelsa Bocci were travelling in Africa and Asia, they each encountered determined entrepreneurs who were seeking a better life for their families – entrepreneurs who needed just a small amount of money to transform their futures. Sometimes, it would simply be the cost of a hairdryer to start a home salon or a small loan to expand a goat herd.

The four friends decided to create a website where entrepreneurs could share their stories and lenders could select a dream to support. While Matt built the website, Jessica engaged with borrowers and took their photographs for their loan profiles. The team would host house parties where, to attend, each guest had to make a loan. As lenders started getting repaid, word of mouth spread and demand grew rapidly. Soon, with an over 97% repayment rate, the numbers spoke for themselves. In the first year, half a million dollars worth of loans were funded. Eventually, people like Oprah and Bill Clinton were advocating for Kiva.

Today, over two million Kiva lenders have funded over USD 1.5 billion in loans and helped nearly 4 million borrowers from 77 countries towards their dreams.

While you may not think you are in a financial position to invest, even small investments can go a long way in countries where the cost of living is comparatively low. Your small loan can provide the resources that a person needs to build an asset that can sustain them financially for a long period of time.

The founders of Kiva learnt this insight from Bangladesh-born Muhammad Yunus. When Muhammad Yunus was in his 30s, he would personally loan small sums of money to impoverished basket-weavers in Bangladesh. He believed that if the poor had access to the financial resources to set up small businesses, they could escape poverty. While traditional moneylenders charged steep interest and expected collateral, Muhammad recognised that this made access to finance next to impossible for destitute individuals. Instead, he started a programme providing micro loans of as little as USD 25 to Bangladeshi women. Borrowers would join lending groups and, with support and transparency among their fellow group members, repay their loans.

In 20 years, Grameen Bank loaned more than USD 6.5 billion, with a repayment rate of over 98%! The Grameen model, initiated in a small Bangladeshi village, has been so successful that is has sparked a global microlending movement and been replicated in over 100 countries. In 2006, Muhammad Yunus was awarded the Nobel Peace Prize.

Earn to donate

Great if you have skills in: Management, medicine, law, finance, sales, real estate and technology

When Warren Buffett was 11 years old, he bought his first stock. By the age of 13, he was filing taxes. At Columbia University, he studied the securities profession under Benjamin Graham, known as the 'father of value investing'. Warren went on to become one of the most successful investors in history, with a net worth of more than USD 100 billion! However, Warren wasn't interested in living a life of luxury. In fact, he still lives in the same home he bought when he was 27 years old for about USD 30,000.

Warren is instead committed to philanthropy. The year 2010 saw he and Bill Gates launch the Giving Pledge, encouraging billionaires to pledge at least half of their wealth to charitable causes. More than 70 billionaires signed the pledge. Warren himself has already given away over USD 45 billion, and in 2020, he pledged to donate more than 99% of his wealth.

"Were we to use more than 1% of my claim checks on ourselves, neither our happiness nor our wellbeing would be enhanced. In contrast, that remaining 99% can have a huge effect on the health and welfare of others."
Warren Buffett

If you have the ability to earn a lot, it is possible that you could make your biggest impact on the world by donating a portion of your earnings to worthy causes. Generally, jobs in management, medicine, law, finance, sales, real estate and technology make more money. But the most important thing is that the job is a good fit with you so that you are able to be exceptional at it – the more exceptional you are, the greater your earning potential. So consider using your skills to make a killing – and then giving to the cause(s) you are passionate about.

In every major region of the world, people who give money to support a cause are happier than those who do not, even after taking into account their own personal financial situation. In fact, donating has about the same impact on happiness as doubled income! Consider calculating the expenses you will need to lead a comfortable life and donating everything you earn over that. In Kenya, the growing middle class gives away more than 20% of its monthly income.

Maximise the good you do by donating to countries and places with the least resources (i.e. the Global South), and selecting initiatives which provide the greatest reduction of suffering. Find charities that meet such criteria by visiting thelifeyoucansave.org. Setting up an automated system to make donations will make this process that much easier.

You can also name charities in your last will – so that, when you leave this earth, you will be leaving it better off than when you entered it. Many people choose to leave 10% of their estate to charity – but you can do much more if you wish. Specify each charity's full name, address and registration number for clarity.

DISCOVER YOUR RESOURCES

"Do what you can, with what you have, where you are."
Theodore Roosevelt

As a part of the Maasai community in Kenya, 11-year-old Richard Turere was told to protect his father's cows from lions that would often come at night. He was determined to do a good job. First, he tried using fire (it just helped the lions see the cows better), then he tried building a scarecrow (they noticed it was always stationary). Then Richard realised that when he moved around the cowshed with a torch at night, lions did not approach. This gave him the idea to design a moving, flashing light that would trick the lions into believing that humans were up and about.

He learnt about electronics by taking apart his mother's radio, then connected lights to a solar panel, an old car battery and an indicator box from a motorcycle (which directs lights to flash to indicate when the motorcycle is about to turn). The result was a simple system of flashing lights that successfully warded off lions, allowing Richard to sleep peacefully at night. Richard's 'lion lights' are so effective, they are now used around Kenya and the world to ward off lions, pumas, tigers, elephants and other animals. Importantly, they have also helped save thousands of wild animals that would otherwise have been killed by people trying to protect their crops and livestock.

What do you need to make a difference? Often, much less than you think! Sometimes we fall into the trap of thinking that in order to have any kind of impact, we need a great deal of money, time or talent. As the stories of the changemakers we have introduced reveal, that isn't always the case. By being creative and resourceful, we can make whatever resources we have go a long way.

Author Alex Banayan insists that there are always 'three ways in': "There's the First Door, where 99% of people wait in line, hoping to get in. There's the Second Door, where billionaires and royalty slip through. But then there is always, *always*, the Third Door. It's the entrance where you have to jump out of line, run down the alley, climb over the dumpster, bang on the door a hundred times, crack open the window, and sneak through the kitchen. But there's always a way in."

If you take stock of what you already have, you might find yourself pleasantly surprised at the resources at your disposal that can help you achieve your goals. Let's explore the resources you already have, or can obtain, in order to make a difference.

Your resources can be divided into six categories:

SKILLS
What can you do well?

PEOPLE
Who can support your goals?

PLACES
What locations do you have access to?

RESOURCES

TIME
When do you have time in your schedule?

TOOLS
What equipment, information and software can you access?

FUNDS
How can you secure funds?

When looking at these items, if your immediate reaction is "I don't have any of these!", don't worry. If you ever feel like you don't have what you need, instead of thinking "I don't have X", think "I don't have X – yet". Often there will be a way for you to get hold of what you need.

We will explore each of these categories one by one, and you might discover that you have more at hand than you think!

Skills

Your skills are those things that you can do well. Everyone has a unique set of skills – and your skills are usually the secret to success in anything you do.

In order to identify your skills, think about what comes naturally to you that might be difficult for others. What do you often get compliments about? What gives you a sense of satisfaction and pride?

Skills can be technical skills (skills specific to a particular task), people skills (skills in relating to others) and execution skills (skills that help with getting things done). Here are some examples of each of these types of skills. This list is by no means exhaustive – you might have skills outside of what is listed here.

Technical skills

- Website or app development
- Building things with your hands
- Knowing multiple languages
- Graphic design
- Painting
- Writing
- Digital art
- Sculpture
- Dancing
- Singing
- Drawing

- Sports
- Electrical work
- Research
- Marketing

People skills

- Empathy
- Social intelligence
- Leadership
- Organising groups
- Public speaking
- Following up with others
- Confidence in speaking truth to power
- Teaching
- Mentoring
- Persuasion
- Being a team player
- Negotiation
- Debate
- Resolving conflicts
- Connecting with a particular group

Execution skills

- Discipline
- Critical analysis
- Strategic thinking
- Problem solving
- Managing crises
- Perseverance
- An eye for excellence
- Organisation
- Honesty
- Enthusiasm
- Curiosity

- Humility
- Optimism
- Humour
- Patience

Can you figure out some of your skills? Write them down here.

Once you have identified your skills, you will be able to put them to use in changing the world!

Activities that are a natural fit with your skills will come easily to you and are more likely to produce results. Since seeing results is encouraging and feels great, you will be motivated to stick with those activities for longer. That matters because the longer you can persevere at something, the greater your chances are of making a huge impact.

Try skill stacking

Skill stacking is the art of combining multiple skills in a strategic way to create a unique set of skills that is more valuable than the sum of its parts. For example, a marketer who has also developed skills in data analysis and graphic design can create more informative and visually appealing campaigns. A software engineer who is skilled in communication and has experience in project management and can be more effective in leading teams and bringing projects to completion. If you have the capacity to do multiple things, combine them. If you can write and speak, use both! If you can sing and play an instrument, use both!

Scott Adams, creator of the Dilbert comic strip, says, "If you think extraordinary talent and a maniacal pursuit of excellence are necessary for success, I say that's just one approach, and probably the hardest. When it comes to skills, quantity often beats quality." He adds, "Success-wise, you're better off being good at two complementary skills than being excellent at one."

Author Darius Foroux agrees: "If you're a one-trick pony, your opportunities are limited. But if you have multiple skills, you're simply more valuable."

Scott Adams says, "I'm a perfect example of the power of leveraging multiple mediocre skills. I'm a rich and famous cartoonist who doesn't draw well. At social gatherings I'm usually not the funniest person in the room. My writing skills are good, not great. But what I have that most artists and cartoonists do not have is years of corporate business experience plus an MBA from Berkeley's Haas School of Business. In the early years of Dilbert my business experience served as the fodder for the comic. Eventually, I discovered that my business skills were essential in navigating Dilbert from a cult hit to a household name. Recapping my skill set: I have poor art skills, mediocre business skills, good but not great writing talent, and an early knowledge of the Internet. And I have a good but not great sense of humour. I'm like one big mediocre soup. None of my skills are world-class, but when my mediocre skills are combined, they become a powerful market force."

Which of your skills complement each other?

Skill gaps

What if you don't have a certain skill that would help you to succeed in working towards your cause(a)? Don't worry, there are ways around this.

First, write down any potential skill gaps in terms of technical, people or execution skills which you feel could become bottlenecks as you work towards having an impact in your chosen cause area(s). Note that you don't have to write down every flaw you think you have, only those gaps that could directly affect your ability to achieve your goals.

If applicable, what are your skill gaps?

Now, let's look at three ways you can bridge these gaps.

Find a workaround

One way to get around skill gaps is to find a workaround! For example, in order to simplify the process of getting something done that you find challenging, you could set up a checklist or system to help you. This could be as simple as making a point to run a spellcheck on your work if you aren't too great at spelling. Often, there are free, online tools that can help you with tasks you may struggle with, from organising projects to managing social media. By breaking tedious activities down to their baby steps, finding supportive tools, and allocating time to get items done, you are going to make it that much easier to check them off your list.

Acquire new skills

Are there skills you would like to build which would contribute towards your ability to change the world? One way to develop such skills is to take on new challenges. This can involve pursuing educational opportunities such as attending workshops or earning certifications, taking on new projects or assignments, or volunteering for opportunities outside your usual scope of work. You can also seek out mentorship and network with others in your field to learn from them. By taking the initiative to develop skills that can fuel your success, you will be better equipped to overcome skill gaps and make an impact.

Find a partner

If you find a task difficult or tedious, it can become a bottleneck in your efforts. For example, if an activity involves talking to strangers, but you prefer to work from behind a laptop and aren't comfortable chatting with people you don't know, you are likely to procrastinate on the activity. The things that stress us out, bore us or drain us can slow our momentum. Something you can do to overcome this is to enlist the support of a complementary partner who has skills in that department. We'll discuss this further in the next section.

People

The people in your life can be an incredible resource to you. They can be a source of valuable assistance, opportunities, connections, and much more.

Let's explore the many types of people who can help you in your journey. If you think you may not be able to access some of these groups of people, don't worry. We'll soon discuss how to go about that!

Complementary people

If your activism involves doing things that you don't enjoy doing or do not have skills in, it's worthwhile to seek support from people who do have those capabilities and interests. For example, if you like to write or code, but don't like to engage with others in groups, you can enlist the support of a partner to do that part. Find someone whose peaks match your valleys, and partner with them. For example, Steve Jobs and Steve Wozniak, the co-creators of the Apple computer, were a complementary pair who were able to achieve far more together by filling in each other's skill gaps. While Jobs had a flair for design and marketing, Wozniak was a computing expert.

In my own work to provide free educational content on meaningful topics to children in Sri Lanka, I have partnered with two friends with complementary skills. While I love to create and therefore design most of Safe Circles' content, my friend Nabila enjoys coordinating with other people. She follows up with our volunteers and translators. Meanwhile, Mihitha is a doctor and a talented teacher and delivers our content to children around the country. Our skillsets interplay neatly, allowing us to have a much bigger impact than any one of us would have had on our own!

Write down the names of people whose skills could be complementary to your own by filling in gaps in your existing skillset:

Experts and inspirations

Experts and inspirations are those people who know a lot about the cause area(s) you are passionate about or who have already made waves in the space. They are recognised authorities on the subject(s). Their efforts can provide you with helpful ideas on how to make the biggest possible impact. Meanwhile, their inputs and endorsements would lend credibility to any efforts you undertake to change the world.

Write down a list of experts and inspirations related to your cause area(s) here. Be sure to consider individuals both locally and internationally.

Talented people

Who are the most talented people you know, or know of? These are the people in your broader network whom you think are exceptional at what they do, whether what they do is accounting, choreography, coordinating groups, graphic design, coding or anything else. To help you recall the exceptional people in your network, refer the list of technical, people and execution skills we looked at under the Skills section. Collaborating with talented people would make your change efforts that much more powerful and effective.

Write down the names of the talented people you can think of here, and what it is that they each do brilliantly.

Influential people

Who are the people you know of who command public attention? These are people whose voices capture interest. They may be successful entrepreneurs, activists, social media influencers, media personalities, business leaders, or everyday individuals with the charisma to light up a room.

Consider people who:

- have big- or medium-sized audiences
- have small but engaged audiences
- are from your region
- are from your country
- are from other countries
- you might know personally
- you hope to know in the future
- may show interest in the cause(s) you support
- have audiences who would be interested in the cause(s) you support

Write down the names of all the relevant influential people you can think of here.

Advocates

Advocates are people who are also passionate about the same cause(s) as you. They may not have had the time or opportunity to act on their interests yet, or they may be acting on them in different ways. They are likely to be enthusiastic supporters of your efforts to change the world. They will speak about your actions with others, share information of yours on social media, and lend a hand in support of the cause.

Write down a list of potential advocates here.

Potential mentors

Mentors can accelerate your progress. A mentor is someone who has experience and expertise in a specific area and can provide you with guidance and support. You can seek out mentors to learn from their experiences, get their advice on how to navigate challenges, and gain insights into how to achieve your goals.

They may be people who:

- know your cause area(s) inside out (see Experts and inspirations)
- are highly skilled in something you want to master
- are doing what you might like to do in the future
- have a lifestyle that inspires you
- have an attitude that inspires you

Write down a list of potential mentors here. Don't worry if you don't know them yet.

Champions

Champions are your biggest supporters. They are the people in your life who believe in you, who provide you with moral and other support, and who would advocate for you and your goals.

Changing the world can be difficult at times. That's why it's important to know your champions and turn to them when you need their help. They may be friends, teachers, parents, coaches, peers, even people you've only had brief encounters with, but who seem to believe in you.

"Asking for help isn't giving up, it's refusing to give up."
Charlie Mackesy

Write down a list of your champions here.

Making connections

So how would you get in touch with the people you don't yet know? Well, it can be easier than you think!

Go where the people are

Who are you trying to connect with? Where do they hang out? Consider if you can join clubs, attend workshops and events, or in other ways network with the individuals whose support you seek, or those who might be able to introduce you to them. Then speak to them directly about yourself, the cause you are passionate about and why you think they would be able to create a huge positive impact by working on the cause with you.

Most people want the world to be a better place, and are likely to want to support a positive cause. Even if there's nothing in it for them, it's quite possible they would be inspired by your efforts and happy to help in whatever capacity they can.

Find their contact details

Many people are accessible via social media, phone or email, and if you take the step of reaching out, you never know who will respond. When Sara Blakely, the founder of Spanx, managed to get her product into a huge retail store, others asked her how she was able to do it. Her simple response? "I called them."

Do some research and try to dig up the contact details of the person you want to get in touch with. Then reach out!

Use the six degrees of separation

In the 1960s, social psychologist Stanley Milgram conducted an experiment to figure out the extent to which all people are connected. He asked a few hundred people to try to get a letter to a target individual they did not know in the city of Boston in the United States. The catch was that they could only send the letter to a friend or acquaintance whom they felt was somehow closer to the target individual than them. He discovered that the letters received had only changed hands around six times before reaching the targeted recipient. This seemed to validate the idea of 'six degrees of separation' – the notion that every person in the world can access every other person via a network of about six links.

But that was the 1960s! In today's hyper-connected, social media-driven world, your capacity for connection is even greater. A 2011 analysis by Facebook found that over 90% of its users are connected by five or fewer steps.

So, if you would like to connect with someone and cannot find a way to reach them, ask yourself who might already know them, or have a better chance of knowing someone who knows them, and reach out to that person. Eventually, with a bit of persistence, you might be able to score an introduction!

Get something done first

Hard-to-reach people are more likely to pay attention if you are able to show them that you have already achieved some level of traction. That might mean showing them a video you have created or a website you have set up, or telling them about the impact your efforts have had thus far, or about other experts you have successfully connected with. By showing people that you have already put in some effort and done the work, your credibility will grow in their eyes. And that, in turn, will boost your chances of getting a response!

Make an offer they can't refuse

For better chances of securing a positive response, consider making the person you seek to connect with an offer which is hard to refuse. For example, suggest a time commitment so small that it would be hard for them to say 'no'. Hopefully, after building rapport with you and having time to get hooked on the cause, they would then be willing to lend more time. You could also volunteer your skills to them free of charge for a period in exchange for their support. Consider what needs and interests the person might have and how you might be able to use your own resources to help them answer the question: 'What's in it for me?'

Places

Next, we come to places. These are the spaces that you have access to. For example, your school, home or local clubs and associations. They can even include the sites of events such as conferences, exhibitions or festivals.

Places are valuable in multiple ways. For example, they can serve as:

- Places to work on your cause
- Places to access particular tools
- Places to advocate for a cause/causes
- Places to showcase your work
- Meeting or event locations
- Networking sites

Social media can also be a powerful place to spread awareness about issues and engage with others. Platforms such as Instagram, TikTok, Twitter, Facebook and LinkedIn have millions of users, making them a powerful force in spreading information and mobilising people. You can use the space to create campaigns, mobilise others to take action, raise funds, and spread the word about the issues that matter to you.

What places do you have access to, or could gain access to?

Sometimes, the places that we use can be full of distractions from our goals. If this applies to any of your places, how can you shape the environment to hide tempting distractions and ensure the space is supportive of your aims?

Write your ideas down below.

Tools

When Easton LaChappelle was 14, he used LEGOs and fishing line to build a robotic arm in his bedroom. He learned to code and controlled the hand with a glove. For his sixteenth birthday, he bought a 3D printer via Kickstarter, a crowdfunding platform for creative projects. He began using the 3D printer to build more human-like arms. The next year, Easton met a small girl at a science fair. While chatting with her parents, he found out that her prosthetic arm had cost tens of thousands of dollars, yet the girl would outgrow it soon. This didn't seem right to Easton. When there were 60 million amputees worldwide, more affordable, accessible and durable solutions were needed.

One year later, Easton secured funding to start a company dedicated to building affordable prosthetic arms. Easton's 3D-printed limbs are lightweight yet durable, and designed to match the user's skin tone.

They are also affordable, selling for about one-tenth the price of other prosthetic devices controlled by muscle movements. Plus, when a child inevitably outgrows their device, the company will upcycle the components and replace it for about half the price of the original. Easton's company has since produced hundreds of prosthetic limbs.

Tools can help you make an impact. They can take many forms, such as:

- Equipment e.g. laptops, tablets, 3D printers, welding machines
- Informational tools e.g. courses, websites, books, documentaries
- Software e.g. Canva, Trello, Ocen Audio

What tools do you have access to? Think outside the box – just because you don't personally own it, doesn't mean you can't access it. Do you have a friend or relative who has one that you can borrow? Does your local library rent it out? Does your school or workplace offer it? Can you access it at the local university or coworking space?

Much of the time, you won't need to access expensive tools to get a job done. With a bit of resourcefulness, you can often find cheap alternatives that work effectively. Take stock of what is available and try to extract as much value as possible.

There are a wealth of free tools available online to support you in achieving your goals. Here are a few examples:

- Naming – Namelix
- Design – Canva
- Website – Google Sites
- Social media – Buffer
- Email – MailerLite
- Project management – ClickUp
- Copywriting – Copy AI
- Proofreading – Grammarly
- Scheduling – Calendly
- Online selling – Gumroad

What are the tools that you have access to, or might be able to gain access to?

Time

Time is arguably the most valuable resource of all. Consider your schedule and identify when you might have time to work on your world-changing efforts. Can you spare some time after school or work? How are your weekends looking – any openings there?

Even a small amount of time invested consistently adds up. Consider that the average person who lives to 80 years will have spent nearly four and a half years of their life eating!

While I was leading a technology startup, I decided to allocate two hours every Sunday towards working on my first book. Those two hours added up. Within two years, I had completed and published the book. Today, I still enjoy the satisfaction of knowing that, every single day, a few new people will pick it up and read my words.

Identify where you might be able to make time in your schedule – then create a recurring event on your calendar for your world-changing projects.

When thinking about the time available to you, also consider the time that you spend doing activities that don't require your full focus. Explore the nitty-gritties of your schedule – you might have more time than you think! For example, the time you spend travelling to work, college or school. Or the time you spend waiting in queues. These pockets of dead time can be very useful.

You can use these small pockets of time to:

- follow up on world-changing projects
- make calls to put pressure on political figures
- send emails to government or corporate entities to petition for change
- learn more about your cause by reading or listening to relevant content
- jot down next steps or big ideas
- send emails to potential allies
- consult mentors

When can you find time in your schedule – and how will you use it?

Funds

Access to funds can be useful as it can help you grow your world-changing projects and get the word out about them so they can reach more people. But don't worry if you don't have money of your own to spare. It's generally a good idea to learn to operate in a lean way. This means getting a lot of value out of a minimal amount of resources. Doing so requires resourcefulness! Get creative and think out of the box about how you can make the most of what you do have at your disposal.

You may not need a lot of funds to make an impact, and if you eventually find that your efforts would benefit from funding, there are several options you can try to secure the resources you need. When you do need some funds, or think it would benefit the growth of your project to put some money behind it, consider these avenues:

Savings

If you have money set aside that you wouldn't miss, you can consider channelling it towards your initiative(s). This might mean investing money to secure resources, hiring someone's services to further your cause, or spending on advertising to promote your campaign.

Loans and donations

When 10-year-old Zymer Umer decided to play her part in tackling Pakistan's waste problem by recycling old newspapers into paper bags, she relied on her father and grandfather for financial support. They helped her buy the materials she needed to convert the newspapers into attractive bags. Eventually, Zymer was selling so many bags via social media that she was able to support charities like SOS Children's Villages, funding items like water coolers and washing machines for the children.

Your friends and family may be willing to chip in money to help you achieve your altruistic goals, so try asking them. Consider reaching out to corporations too to seek their support. You can make a compelling case by describing what you expect to achieve with the funds you seek.

Crowdfunding

When Italian-born couple Francesca Cavallo and Elena Favilli were growing up, they didn't have books that showcased female role models. They decided to change that for the next generation by creating a book, Good Night Stories for Rebel Girls, which would showcase the stories of 100 incredible women achievers, along with beautiful illustrations by female artists from around the world. In order to make their vision a reality, they conducted a crowdfunding campaign on two websites – Kickstarter and Indiegogo – and ended up raising USD 1 million with the help of 20,000 supporters from more than 70 countries. It became the most and fastest funded book in crowdfunding history. The two editions of Good Night Stories for Rebel Girls have now sold more than 2.5 million copies worldwide. They continue to inspire girls around the world to follow their big and bold dreams.

Crowdfunding is a way of securing the funds to undertake a project from several people who would like to see the project achieve its goals. The beauty of crowdfunding is that it enables a large crowd of passionate people to make small contributions which ultimately add up to an impressive sum.

You can use an online crowdfunding website to facilitate the process of crowdfunding. Set up a page on the platform that describes your project, its goals, resource requirements, funding goal and timeframe. If you can, include a video on your page. You can also offer exclusive rewards to people who donate specific amounts, such as customised gifts related to your cause. Then make use of social media and email to share the link to your crowdfunding page far and wide!

Partnerships

Many organisations like partnering with good initiatives as it helps them build their own reputations while providing a social or environmental benefit. You may be able to partner with an organisation which can provide you with the resources you would otherwise need funding for. Consider which organisations have goals that align with those of your cause(s) and reach out to them.

Grants

There are many organisations that provide grants to people who are trying to change the world. Do an online search to identify which organisations offer grants to projects in your cause area and/or from your region. Next, prepare a proposal.

Your proposal would typically include a description of your project, the team behind it, what has been done so far and any successes achieved, what you hope to do in the future, and the funding required. Be sure to explain the impact you expect your project to have, and include specific numbers wherever possible. Be sure to follow any guidelines provided by the organisation offering the grant.

Investments

Sarah Paiji Yoo wanted to cut single-use plastics from her life after learning about how much of it ends up in the oceans and environment. Unfortunately, everything seemed to come in single-use plastic packaging. She decided to partner with Syed Naqvi from Pakistan to create the Blueland set of tablet-based hand soaps and cleaning products. These simple scented tablets dissolve in water, converting it into cleaning liquid, so you never need to buy plastic-packaged cleaning products again.

As soon as they had a viable product, the pair applied to appear on Shark Tank, a TV show where entrepreneurs can pitch for investment. They prepared extensively – and it paid off. They secured an investment of USD 270,000, and within a year, they had done over USD 15 million in sales. Today, over a million households use Blueland products in place of those that come in plastic packaging.

Investors are individuals who are willing to put their money behind initiatives which they feel have strong potential. If you know someone who is interested in societal or environmental development and likely to have money that they could put towards your initiative, consider making a pitch for their investment.

Practice describing what you intend to do clearly and powerfully within one or two minutes. This 'elevator pitch' (so called as it should be short enough to be delivered during the time it takes to ride an elevator) will be your initial tool to grab the potential investor's interest and hopefully secure more of their time.

If they are interested, set a date and time at their convenience to provide them with more information. At this meeting, tell them about the nature of your project, what makes your team the best team to execute it, what you have done and achieved thus far, your plans going forward, what each step entails, the resources you need, and the funding required.

If you are a social enterprise, you will also want to share what you expect to earn over the next five years, what percentage of the company you would give them for their investment, and what financial return they can expect. Describe the expected social/environmental impact, including specific numbers wherever possible, and prepare for any questions you think they might have. A slide deck is likely to help you communicate these clearly – if so, be sure to use one.

Practice delivering your pitch several times in front of family and friends and take note of feedback. If you are seeking a large investment, you may not get a second chance to make an impression and secure the funding you want. Be prepared to make the most of it!

How much money do you think you need to make the impact you want?

What avenues will you explore to secure the funds you need?

One more vital resource

Changing the world isn't easy. That's why there's one more vital resource we need to discuss. It's mental health. Your mental health is an important resource to take care of as you go about the important work of making the world a better place. Here are some ways to care for your mental health.

Rest and practice self-care

In your quest to make a difference, you are likely to encounter times when you feel overwhelmed, fed up and exhausted. When that happens, take time to rest. Often, it will actually be better for your own cause(s) that you take a break. Taking a break helps you regain your energy so that you can get back into the vital work of making a difference with vigour and enthusiasm.

If you don't rest and practice self-care, you risk burning out. That isn't good for you *or* for your cause(s). So, when you start to feel overwhelmed, take it as a cue to slow down. Take time to rest and to practice self-care in the ways you most enjoy.

Here are some ideas on how to practice self-care:

- Take a nap
- Write in a journal
- Practice a hobby
- Exercise or play a sport
- Meet friends or have a call with a loved one
- Play with a small child or a pet
- Spend time in nature
- Go for a walk
- Meditate

Take as long as you need to feel refreshed and renewed.

What are your favourite ways to rest and practice self-care?

Find your allies

If you are taking on a large project, don't try to do it all alone. That would be a recipe for burnout. Finding allies in your quest is a valuable way to protect your mental health. Identify people who can help you and enlist their support. Having like-minded people in your life gives you a sounding board to vent, brainstorm, plan and act. This could ultimately make your project better and more sustainable in the long run. When you encounter challenges, having a support structure to help you deal with them can mean everything.

Whom will you count on when you need support?

Recall your past successes

Remembering what you have achieved in the past can help you feel motivated to keep going when times are tough.

What are you proud of having achieved so far?

Celebrate small wins

Because you are tackling very big and important issues, it can sometimes feel like your progress isn't adequate. That's why it's important to celebrate the small wins on your journey towards making a difference.

A Harvard study found that daily journaling about small successes boosts creativity and motivation. Recording your progress, plans, benefits and rewards (in any format) boosts your capacity to keep going.

So recognise your mini wins, journal about them, tell others about what you've achieved, and mark the occasion with a small celebration or personal treat. The way you treat yourself doesn't have to be fancy –

it could simply be a lunch outing with a friend, a slab of dark chocolate, or an episode of your favourite TV show. The important thing is to acknowledge that you are doing important work and your mini milestones deserve to be celebrated!

What are the milestones you will celebrate – and how?

Let go of perfectionism

Avoid stressing out over whether or not what you're doing is 'perfect'. If you aren't willing to do or release anything that isn't perfect, you may struggle to get anything done. In order to get your initiative going, you might need to let go of some degree of perfectionism. An imperfect initiative that has been released into the world is always more valuable than something perfect which will never be available to the world.

Be ready to create a 'shoddy first draft' – something imperfect but with all the essential components in place. You can always improve on it later. Set yourself a deadline and make your initiative as good as it can be until then – then take a deep breath and release it into the world. Remember, done is better than perfect!

Resources in action

Brainstorm

Now that you have explored your skills, people, places, tools, time and funds, you are ready to start brainstorming how you can use these in combination to make an impact in your cause area.

How can your skills be applied towards the cause(s)?

How can you engage the people you identified in support of the cause(s)?

How can you make use of the places you identified to benefit the cause(s)?

How can you make use of the tools you identified in support of the cause(s)?

How can you spend your available time in a way that benefits the cause(s)?

How can you use funding in ways that support the cause(s)?

Synergy is the name given to the phenomenon where two things work together to produce an effect that is greater than the sum of their parts. It is often presented as '1 + 1 > 2'. Consider if there are ways in which you can combine your resources (skills, people, places, tools, time and funds) to produce an even greater impact.

Write down any ideas you have below.

Make a plan

Having brainstormed how your resources can be applied towards your cause, it's time to take action!

Write down in as much detail as possible what you intend to do to make a difference and how you will go about it.

Now write down when you plan to get it done. Try to make this a realistic date, but also one that feels close. You are more likely to procrastinate on a goal if it bleeds into the following calendar week, month or year.

Imagine the above date has arrived but you were not able to achieve your goal. Why do you think that might have happened? What could get in the way of achieving your goal?

How will you tackle these potential hurdles? What can you do to prevent them from derailing your plan?

INFLUENCE AND INSPIRE

*"Storytellers are the most powerful people in the world.
They shape culture, politics and values."*
Steve Jobs

Change occurs when you can influence the behaviour of the people around you. There are two main groups of people you could choose to influence:

1. People in the community
   These are usually the largest group of people and the people most affected by the issues. If you can encourage them to better understand and act in favour of important issues, you can have a big impact.

2. People in power
   These are the people who have the authority to make or put into action decisions that affect others. They may be politicians (at all levels of government), company heads or even school principals. If you can encourage them to take important issues seriously, you can have a big impact.

Your work as a social activist and creative activist will be directed towards influencing these two groups of people. For best results, you will need to have a solid communication strategy. Let's start planning.

Know your audience

One of the oldest social science theories is the Diffusion of Innovation Theory, developed by Everett Rogers. It was created to show how ideas spread through societies. It describes how different groups within a society are more likely than others to adopt an idea. Each group must be approached differently and at different times in order to roll out an idea as rapidly as possible across a society. The theory has worked in many fields including social work, criminal justice, agriculture, and public health.

These are the five different segments of society described by the model:

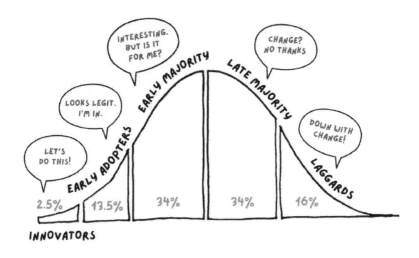

1. *Innovators*

   This is the smallest group of people. These are people who are eager for change and curious about new ideas. They are likely to quickly connect with the idea and fully embrace it almost as soon as they hear about it. Not much has to be done to convince them – simply make them aware of the idea. In fact, they may already be championing it!

2. *Early adopters*

   This is the next smallest group of people. They will usually hear about the idea from innovators. These people would be largely inclined towards the idea. They already understand the need for change and are very comfortable adopting new ideas. Instead of trying hard to convince this group, you simply need to show them exactly what they can do to act in support of the idea.

3. *Early majority*

   This group of people will adopt an idea once they have enough exposure to hearing about it from the innovators and early adopters and have some degree of confidence that it works. They are more likely to adopt the idea than the average person, but they may need to see some evidence or success stories first.

4. *Late majority*

   This group of people is generally sceptical about change. They would only adopt an idea after it has been tried, tested and adopted by the majority of the population. In order to be convinced, they would need hard data on how many others have adopted the idea and on the success of the idea.

5. *Laggards*

   This is a very conservative group of people that is resistant to change. Sometimes, they actually benefit from keeping the status quo as it is, making them all the more resistant. In order to convince them, you might illustrate to them the risks to them of failure to change, show them data and statistics, and engage the support of the other segments of people.

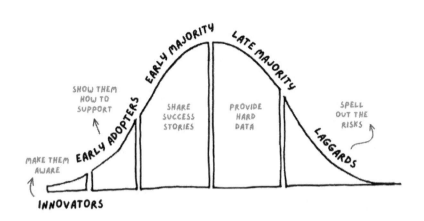

In order to make effective progress, first aim to get the innovators, early adopters and early majority on board with an idea before you seek to convince the late majority and the laggards. Following this strategy would make your communication efforts more successful.

If you try to convince the change-resistant late majority and laggards first, you may find yourself beating your head against a wall and get burnt out quickly. Since your energy is not infinite, spend it in the most productive way. Work your way strategically through the innovation diffusion curve. The initial wins of getting the innovators and early adopters on board will give you the energy (and support) you need to begin to tackle the early and late majorities and, eventually, the laggards.

Can you think of examples of people or organisations that fit into these groups when it comes to embracing your cause(s)?

Innovators:

Early adopters:

Early majority:

Late majority:

Laggards:

Know what to share

When planning how to get people to support your cause(s), keep in mind these seven key factors that would influence them:

1. *Understandability*
   How easy is your idea to understand?

2. *Actionability*
   How easy is your idea to apply or act on?

3. *Benefit*
   How much better is your idea compared with what it would replace?

4. *Alignment*
   How well does your idea align with their values, needs and experiences?

5. *Success*
   Can the impacts of implementing the idea be seen and felt?

6. *Testability*
   Can the idea be tested before making a commitment to adopt it?

7. *Risk*
   How do the risks of failing to adopt your idea compare with the risks of adopting it?

When you are communicating with your audiences, plan how you can show them that your idea is easy to understand and apply, is an improvement on the status quo, aligns with their values, experiences and needs, has proven positive impacts, can be tested, and represents a lower risk than sticking to the status quo.

Use the space below to brainstorm along these lines:

How can you communicate your idea in a way that is easy to understand?

What easy actions can a person take to start to apply your idea?

Why is your idea much better than the status quo?

In what ways does your idea align with the values, needs and experiences of your target audiences?

Innovators:

Early adopters:

Early majority:

Late majority:

Laggards:

What are the positive impacts of implementing the idea that can be seen and felt?

How can your idea be tested before your audience makes a commitment to adopt it?

What are the risks of failing to adopt your idea?

Design your messaging

Now that we have discussed how to tackle different audiences and what content to share with them, let's consider how to design our messages to have the best possible impact.

Providing hope and inspiring action

One of the reasons many people avoid engaging with cause-related material is that it can often feel very heavy. It can be saddening and infuriating to think about the major problems in the world, and viewers sometimes feel helpless learning about the scale of the issues.

Therefore, while you are creating awareness about the size and importance of the causes that matter to you, consider also providing information on what is being done to help further those causes, and what individuals interacting with the material can immediately do upon learning about them – for example, signing a petition or placing a call to an elected official.

By providing a clear avenue for hope and action, you help audiences feel more comfortable engaging with cause-related material, and also give them clear direction to support the cause(s) you are passionate about.

Communicating with emotion

It's absolutely correct to feel anger and resentment that not enough is being done to address an issue. If you are a victim of the issue, it can be even more upsetting. Your emotions are valid. I don't agree with the idea that people should not express anger, frustration, disappointment or hurt when talking about important issues that affect themselves and others. It is not fair for people who face discrimination, for example, to be told that in addition to suffering through discrimination, they must also maintain a calm and positive demeanour when dealing with people who deny or undermine their suffering.

I personally know how upset I feel when people in my home country of Sri Lanka seem oblivious to or deny the painful challenges that are faced by women, minorities or LGBTQIA+ persons in the country. My pain often shows up as frustration and anger. I might feel the urge to raise my voice or to criticise. And yet, if my objective is to convince the other person to support my cause, I know intellectually that this is an ineffective way to do so. The moment I make another person feel defensive, I make it much harder for them to accept my ideas. Despite this knowledge, I am human and I know that the frustration and anger I feel are symptoms of how much I care about these issues and the people affected by them. My emotions are valid.

Yet, in order to make the largest possible positive impact towards the causes I care about, I try to adopt a strategic approach in my communication. When communicating about a cause, I try to remember that my goal is to achieve progress for that cause. Therefore, when possible (and it isn't always possible!), I try to tactfully provide information that can gently guide the audience towards a better understanding of the issue. This means moderating the tone of my voice to one that does not elicit defensiveness, avoiding the use of polarising labels or loaded words, asking strategic questions, and sharing stories, statistics and examples that clarify my views.

When I adopt this approach, I often find my audience to be more receptive to my views than I ever expected – which ultimately supports my cause. That said, I'm no saint and, sometimes, with particularly ignorant and hostile audiences, I simply do away with communication strategy!

When you are determining how to present your ideas, consider adjusting your communication strategy to suit the receptiveness of the audience. With audiences that are more receptive to your ideas (e.g. innovators and early adopters), expressing frustration and anger can actually be very effective. However, with audiences who are sceptical or resistant, such language can sometimes work against the cause. Therefore, plan how to strategically engage with different audience groups.

Here are some research-backed tips for engaging emotion to secure more interest and contribution towards your cause(s):

- Highlight the plight on one person, not masses of people, as it's easier to empathise with an individual than a crowd.
- As Martin Luther King Jr. did in his speech, to prompt effective action, draw attention to the victims of injustice, not the perpetrators.
- Prompt people to reflect on their good fortune as it increases willingness to contribute to the common good.
- Rouse emotion as emotionally roused people (e.g. those asked to think about babies) tend to give twice as much as those in neutral emotional states.
- Highlight others' contributions to the cause(s) – since humans are social animals, people are more likely to contribute if they know others are doing so.
- If you are seeking donations, you can boost the total amount of donations by using wording that implies even small donations are valid (e.g. 'Every little bit helps').
- Use a red donation box or webpage as the colour red suggests urgency and thus promotes giving.

Tackling hatred and misinformation

Hate speech can have real-world consequences, spreading discrimination, violence and hostility. You might come across hate speech and false information being shared in real life or on social media. Speaking up against it can help to create a culture of accountability. When we call out hate speech and misinformation, we send a message that it is not acceptable. This can motivate others to do the same and create a ripple effect of positive change.

When speaking up, use clear and direct language. Never engage in name-calling or personal attacks as this can take away from your message and make it easier for others to dismiss your argument. Instead, provide evidence to back up your arguments – this can help to counter misinformation and show that you are not just expressing an opinion, but presenting facts. Amplify the voices of those who are impacted by hate speech and misinformation. Share their stories and experiences, and elevate their voices.

If you believe that the other person may be open to constructive dialogue, consider speaking to them privately, for example with a personal message or call. Sharing the reasons you believe the content shared is harmful and asking for the poster's perspective can sometimes be more effective in changing their views than a public confrontation. When the conversation is private, the other party may feel less inclined to defend their ego.

On the other hand, public responses can be valuable when they show others that hate speech and misinformation is not acceptable and will not be tolerated. It can also sometimes lead to more reasoned responses from the other party as they know their words are publicly visible.

You can make the choice of whether to engage privately or publicly based on what you know about the person sharing the post or comment. If you know them already or they seem like they may be reasonable, consider engaging privately. Also consider how damaging the remark or post is – if it is more damaging, consider engaging publicly to create more accountability.

Avoid engaging with individuals who are not open to constructive dialogue. This can be counterproductive and may only serve to escalate the situation. Instead, consider reporting harmful content to authorities (for example, to the leader of an organisation the person is part of, to the social media platform where the content was posted, or the admin of a WhatsApp group where the comment was made).

Confrontations can be emotionally draining, so be sure to engage your friends in providing you with emotional support as you go about fighting the good fight!

Keep in mind these (lightly edited) words of Theodore Roosevelt: "It is not the critic who counts; not the person who points out how the strong one stumbles, or where the doer of deeds could have done them better. The credit belongs to the one who is actually in the arena, whose face is marred by dust and sweat and blood; who strives valiantly; who errs, who comes short again and again, because there is no effort without error and shortcoming; but who does actually strive to do the deeds; who knows great enthusiasms, the great devotions; who spends themself in a worthy cause; who at the best, knows in the end the triumph of high achievement, and who at the worst, if they fail, at least fails while daring greatly, so that their place shall never be with those cold and timid souls who neither know victory nor defeat."

Amplify your impact

"Whatever you're thinking, think bigger."
Tony Hsieh

As you go about changing the world, consider how you can scale your efforts to make the biggest impact possible. Let's explore some avenues you can take to expand your reach.

Combine forces

Sometimes, a changemaker may be so excited to execute an idea that they jump into it without first taking the time to look around. There will often be multiple people and organisations also working in support of the same cause. Sometimes, their objectives and activities will overlap.

By identifying existing initiatives and collaborating with them, you may find that you don't have to reinvent the wheel but can instead build on what has already been achieved. Collaboration allows you to combine several unique strengths to create something greater than the sum of its parts. It can allow you to pool your skills, people, places, tools and time, rapidly growing the reach of your efforts!

Provide resources

When Israel-born filmmaker Leslee Udwin travelled to India to create a film about a vicious act of gender-based violence and the thousands of people protesting against it, she decided that it would be the last film she would ever make. She decided to instead make it her life's mission to provide the children of the world with an education in compassion. So she developed the Think Equal curriculum – a 30-week programme for three- to six-year-olds featuring 30 books, lesson plans and other materials to provide a deep grounding in the concepts of equality, inclusion and wellbeing. Teachers in 25 countries across six continents have used these resources to instil compassion, empathy and understanding in children. As a result, today, Leslee's resources have positively impacted over 240,000 children.

In order to scale your impact, you might choose to provide others with the resources they need to support a cause. This might look like creating a database of politicians' contact information so that anyone can petition them for change, or developing an application which helps any individual become an eco-warrior by offsetting their carbon footprint. In effect, instead of taking on the burden of singlehandedly supporting the cause, you can accelerate your impact by equipping an army of individuals to fight for the cause.

Make it digital

Compared with anything physical, digital creations can be shared instantly, reaching a large number of people in a short space of time. By making something available digitally, you give it the chance to explode in popularity using the Internet's network effects.

If the idea you have in mind is not a digital one, consider if you can introduce a digital angle to it. Can you make it available via a website, create a mobile application, live stream it, deliver it as a podcast or video series, or share it far and wide with a creative social media post? By making your message or initiative available in a digital format, you can potentially reach many more people in your community, and even the world.

Improve it with feedback

One of the important things to figure out with a social initiative is whether or not it would connect with its audience. To test this, seek out honest feedback from those who would be your audience. Demand critical comments from friends, family, and strangers as well. By doing so, you will have the chance to iron out any kinks that might stop people from embracing your efforts and sharing them with everyone they know.

"Most people want to be nice, so they shy away from sharing negative feelings. Force your friends and family to tell you the thing about your product that they hate. Ask people why they aren't using it."
Alex Groth, co-founder of Tab for a Cause

Try to show potential users or participants what the idea, product, service or initiative would look like, with drawings, prototypes or samples. These need not be very sophisticated, as long as they give the person a better idea of what would be on offer.

To get feedback, ask in person or use questionnaires. Ask specific questions about what they like and dislike, what might stop them from using it, the locations where they would expect to access it, and if applicable, how much they would pay for it. Take note of their feedback and use it to improve your idea.

And if the feedback is poor across the board, don't be afraid to drop the idea and go back to the drawing board. Your next idea might be a gamechanger! Remember, the goal here is to produce something that has the highest chance of making a large positive impact.

Spread the word

Research shows that simply finding out about another person's cause-related efforts can encourage others to behave more generously themselves. So don't be shy about showcasing your efforts – doing so will benefit the world. A series of small pushes can help give your efforts a much wider reach.

Let's explore how the founders of Tab for a Cause, a tool that has raised over USD 1.5 million for charity, grew with simple tactics and by embracing feedback:

In 2010, when Kevin Jennison and Alex Groth were juniors in college, they recognised that they enjoyed working together on projects and promised to swap ideas. One idea in particular resonated with both of them. It was the idea to create a web browser extension that would show users a few advertisements every time they opened a new browser tab – with the ad revenue then donated to non-profits like Save The Children. This extension would allow people to make real charitable donations, simply by surfing the web! They called it 'Tab for a Cause'.

Kevin and Alex spent their winter break studying coding from web tutorials. After creating the first draft of their web extension, they asked 30 of their closest friends and family for honest feedback. Once they had the validation that the idea was a good one, and fixed the key issues that had been pointed out, they were ready to launch their tool. They did so by using Facebook to post about it on their own profiles – and those of everyone they knew. Then they encouraged their friends and family to do the same.

This was the simple message they sent out: 'Hello! My friend and I are starting a web-based non-profit called Tab for a Cause, which lets you raise money for charity by surfing the web. We realize it sounds too good to be true, but we assure you it isn't! It takes less than a minute to get involved – visit www.tabforacause.org. To help spread the word, please like us on Facebook and pass this on to any friends! Thanks so much for your help!' This got them their first 200-300 new users.

To grow further, they asked each of their college newspapers to include a small article about the tool, and posted about 100 flyers in the campus dorms and bathrooms. This got them a few more hundred users.

They then posted about the tool in online forums, and a small-scale YouTuber featured their tool in a video. This video was in turn featured by a large charity event, drawing in 700 new users and helping them cross the 1,000 users mark.

More recently, Tab for a Cause has started experimenting with targeting people interested in specific causes. For example, by promoting 'Tab for Cats' to encourage cat-lovers to open tabs to donate towards the rehabilitation of shelter cats. Today, Tab for a Cause has over 200,000 users and has raised over USD 1.5 million for charity, with no signs of slowing down.

Like Kevin and Alex, seek out simple and creative ways of getting the word out about your initiative. Try multiple avenues and double down on whatever works best.

Build a community

Starting a community can multiply your efforts. The more people who understand, care about and work on critical causes, the greater the potential impact. By engaging like-minded people in your cause(s), you have far more ammunition beyond your own time and energy. By turning your message into a movement, you expand its reach as every new participant has the capacity to influence many others.

By creating a community around your cause, you can also attract more attention from people in positions of authority who would take your message more seriously when it has support from a large number of people.

In order to start a community around your cause, consider creating a sign-up form for volunteers, initiating a club or society, or creating a WhatsApp or Facebook group. Introduce clear objectives and brainstorm activities for the group to engage in to further the cause.

Activate influencers

Influential people can shine a very bright spotlight on your cause(s). With a pre-existing and often passionate audience, influencers can rapidly get a lot more people engaged with your cause. Tap the networks of people who are well-networked – it can trigger a flood of valuable attention. See the section on People in the Discover Your Resources chapter to learn more about identifying and reaching out to influencers.

Inject funding

Gaining funding for your efforts can help you accelerate success by empowering you to produce more and reach more people. Once you think you are ready to effectively use funding to make an impact, go back to our section on Funds in the Discover Your Resources chapter and explore your options.

Translate it

Of the 8 billion people in the world, English is the first language of fewer than 500 million. By translating your material into several languages, you have the potential to reach a much larger audience. Identify the most widely used languages in your targeted markets and prioritise those when getting translations done.

My first book, 'Cheat Sheets for Life', aims to help people lead happier and healthier lives by compiling research on optimising different areas of life into one concise handbook. In order to make it accessible to more people, I have worked with translators to make it available in German, Spanish, Italian, French and Turkish.

Use humour

Humour is a powerful way to connect with people – and to inspire them to talk about something and share it with others. Consider Zack Brown's Potato Salad Project. This was a quirky campaign on the crowdfunding website Kickstarter which declared that it was raising funds to – wait for it – make a potato salad! The crowdfunding page read: "Basically I'm just making potato salad. I haven't decided what kind yet." Zack pledged to say the names of funders out loud while making the potato salad. The comical campaign went viral and raised over USD 55,000, which Zack used for a charity event benefitting hunger relief organisations. Explore how you too can use humour within your own efforts to engage and connect with more people.

RECOMMENDED RESOURCES

Here are some resources to help changemakers like you make a difference today. Many of these tools have been created by the changemakers discussed in this book. Unfortunately, a few of the resources are not available in all countries. If that's the case for your homeland, consider starting a similar offering in your own country.

7 Cups
Volunteer to listen to people who need a friendly ear
www.7cups.com

80,000 Hours
Learn how to select and find a career to change the world
80000hours.org

Be My Eyes
Remotely help visually impaired people undertake daily tasks
www.bemyeyes.com

Blueland
Use these eco-alternatives to disposable cleaning products
www.blueland.com
*Not available in all countries

Change.org
Start an online petition for a cause you care about
change.org

Forest
Plant trees by staying off your phone and being productive
www.forestapp.cc

Free Rice
Donate rice to hungry kids by playing trivia games
play.freerice.com

Giving Pledge
Pledge to donate 10% of your income to high-impact causes
www.givingwhatwecan.org/pledge

Good On You
Check if brands are socially and environmentally conscious
goodonyou.eco
*Not available in all countries

HappyCow
Find vegan and vegetarian-friendly restaurants worldwide
www.happycow.net

Imperfect Foods
Fight food waste and save cash when buying produce
www.imperfectfoods.com
*Not available in all countries

Kiva
Give loans to micro-entrepreneurs from around the world
www.kiva.org

Tab for a Cause
Make donations to causes simply by browsing the web
tab.gladly.io

Too Good to Go
Prevent food waste while getting great deals on food items
www.toogoodtogo.com
*Not available in all countries

The Life You Can Save
Learn about effective giving and download the free book
www.thelifeyoucansave.org

Safe Circles
Deliver free workshop materials to give kids better lives
www.safecircles.lk

Stand for Trees
Calculate your carbon footprint and buy credits to offset it
standfortrees.org

TEMPLATE TOOLKIT

Call to a politician

"Hello, I would like to make a comment to [elected official's name] about [problem or policy]."

"My name is [your full name], and I live in [your town]. I'm calling to urge [elected official's name] to support laws that [fix the problem you are calling about - explain that here]. I care about this because [reason]."

Letter to a politician

[Your address (to receive responses)]

[Politician's address]

[Date]

[Subject]

Dear [representative's name],

My name is [your name], and I am a constituent from [your town]. I am writing to you because I want to know what you will do to support [cause]. This is important because [how the issue affects you and others]. I am writing to urge you, as an elected official, to [action(s) expected].

I believe that in making these changes, you would demonstrate integrity and win loyalty while doing your part to support [cause]. If you do take action, please let me know.

I look forward to your response.

Sincerely,

[Your name]

Letter to a company

[Your address (to receive responses)]

[Company address]

[Date]

[Subject]

Dear [company representative's name/title],

I am writing to you about [concern]. This is a vital issue because [details about the cause].

I hope your organisation will take the following steps to improve this situation: [Action(s) expected]

I believe that in making these changes, your organisation could win stronger brand respect and greater customer loyalty while doing your part to support [cause]. If you do take action, please let me know. I would be happy to champion your efforts among my friends and family via social media.

I look forward to your response.

Sincerely,

[Your name]

Petition

[Headline with emotional appeal]

[Details about the issue]

This is not okay! It's time to make a change! Sign our petition to demand [action(s) expected and by whom].

Fundraiser

[Headline with emotional appeal]

Join our campaign to raise funds for [cause]. This is important because [impacts of the issue].

This is how your donation can make a difference:

[Details on how funds will be used]

Here's how to donate:

[Details on how to donate]

Every little bit helps! Thank you for supporting [cause].

Campaign slogans

Animal rights

- No excuse for animal abuse
- Don't act blindly, treat animals kindly
- Big or small, be kind to all
- We are the generation that ends animal exploitation
- Speak for those who have no voice

- Animals are friends, not food
- Love animals, not just pets
- Animals are our friends – we don't eat our friends
- Factory farming causes more greenhouse gas emissions than all transport combined
- If you think vegans are loud, listen to the screams in a slaughterhouse

Democracy

- I've seen smarter cabinets at IKEA
- Can we please put smart people in charge now?
- Words are good, actions are better
- Your vote is your voice
- Every election is determined by the people who show up – Larry Santo
- The right to vote is the basic right, without which all others are meaningless – Lyndon B. Johnson
- People should not fear their government, governments should fear their people – Alan Moore
- The master's tools will never dismantle the master's house – Audre Lorde
- In a time of universal deceit, telling the truth becomes a revolutionary act
- Do you hear the people sing? It is the music of a people who will not be slaves again!

Disability rights

- Disability rights are human rights
- Nothing about us without us!
- See the ability, not the disability
- Our differences do not define us
- My ability is stronger than my disability
- The world needs all kinds of minds
- Not all disabilities are visible
- Human rights are not optional
- Look beyond disability and see the person

- Inclusion is within everyone's ability

Environment

- There is no Planet B
- Save the Earth – it's where I keep all my stuff
- Denial is not a policy
- Don't be a fossil fool
- I'm not cool with global warming
- Why should I clean my room if the world is a mess?
- The Earth is getting hotter than my imaginary boy/girlfriend
- I'd be at school if the earth was cool
- It's getting hot in here so take off all your coals
- System change not climate change

Inclusivity

- We are all human
- Diversity is beautiful
- No one is illegal
- Inhale equality, exhale hate
- Nobody's free until everybody's free
- We are stronger together
- Diversity is a fact, inclusion is an act
- What a beautiful day to respect people's rights
- Society: Be yourself. Society: No, not like that.
- Our ability to reach unity in diversity will be the beauty and the test of our civilisation – Mahatma Gandhi

LGBTQIA+ rights

- Love wins
- Love is love
- Love is never wrong
- Love has no gender
- Love is a human right
- Proud to be an ally
- Never apologise for who you are

- My existence is not a political agenda
- Respect my existence or expect my resistance
- Being yourself is never the wrong thing to do

Peace

- Make art, not war, make music, not missiles
- Use words, not weapons
- Our blood, your hands
- Silence is violence
- People for peace
- War is costly, peace is priceless
- Anything war can do, peace can do better
- In a world where you can be anything, be kind
- There is no way to peace, peace is the way
- Peace is its own reward

Reproductive rights

- Trust women
- Bans off our bodies
- Our bodies matter too
- Not your body, not your business
- Sugar, spice and reproductive rights
- I'm not ovary-acting
- Keep your filthy laws off my silky drawers
- Not your body. Not your life. Not your choice.
- You can't ban abortion. You can only ban safe abortions.
- Restricting access to abortions does not reduce the number of abortions – World Health Organisation

Women's rights

- Women's rights are human rights
- Women hold up half the sky
- Dear future daughter, this one is for you
- Girls just wanna have fun…damental rights
- I will not go quietly back to the 1950's

- A woman's place is in the resistance
- Well-behaved women seldom make history
- My arms are tired from holding this sign since the 70's
- Real men support women's rights
- Women belong in all places where decisions are made – Ruth Bader Ginsberg

Other

- Evil prevails when good people do nothing
- Sorry for the inconvenience, we are trying to change the world
- So bad, even introverts are here
- History has its eyes on you
- This is what democracy looks like
- You messed with the wrong generation
- My outrage can't fit on this sign
- If you're not outraged, you're not paying attention
- I need to be able to tell my children I did not stay silent
- If you are neutral in situations of injustice, you have chosen the side of the oppressor – Desmond Tutu

LET'S DO THIS

Congratulations, you are now equipped to change the world. You've learnt from changemakers from across the globe, studied strategies for making a difference and come up with a plan to convert your ideas into reality. Now all that's left to do is to take action! If this book has inspired you to do your part to build a better world, write to me at hi@cheatsheets.life and tell me about your efforts. I would love to hear about them!

And if you would like to help turn more everyday people into changemakers, here are a few more things you can do:

Share your rating or review

 Your rating and review can encourage others to read the book and become changemakers too. To review and inspire more people to change the world, visit www.amazon.com/dp/B0CP2YCP68 or scan this QR code.

Gift 'Changemaker'

 We need as many changemakers as possible working to build a better world. If you enjoyed Changemaker and would like to gift someone else a copy, visit www.amazon.com/dp/B0CP2YCP68 or scan this QR code.

ALSO BY THE AUTHOR

Cheat Sheets for Life

Cheat Sheets for Life is a concise handbook of science-backed advice on 17 dimensions of life, from health to money to leadership to relationships.

In Cheat Sheets for Life, you'll learn:

- How playing the game 'Tetris' can protect your mood
- The superfood that is "the most important dietary predictor of lifespan"
- Why you don't need to have 8 glasses of water a day – and what to do instead
- The one factor that can predict your relationship satisfaction 10 years from now
- Why using all your vacation days boosts your chance of getting a raise
- Why you should keep a cute baby's photo in your wallet
- And 740+ more valuable insights!

Cheat Sheets for Life aims to be the last book you'll ever need to improve your life. Using time-tested research, it strives to give even the busiest individual a foolproof guide to an optimised life.

To learn more about the book, scan the code or visit amazon.com/dp/B08TYQ4HH8.

The Utopia Playbook

The Utopia Playbook reveals the secrets of an ideal world based on the real-life efforts of the most inspiring nations. It will take you on a journey to the world's most impressive countries, and show you what it takes to make real change.

A utopia full of happiness, health and abundance might sound like a pipe dream. But, if you look closely enough, the world is already full of utopias. The Utopia Playbook explores the countries that top the world's indices in all the metrics that matter. Tap the secrets of:

- Finland, which is the world's happiest country
- Hong Kong, which has the longest life expectancy
- Bhutan, which is carbon neutral
- Spain, which is the biggest organ donor
- France, which has the least food waste
- And dozens more countries that hold the keys to an ideal world

Discover where people can safely leave their babies in strollers by the street and which nation has doubled its GDP – while halving its carbon emissions. Explore how one country is creating a nicotine-free generation and where drone technology is used to grow new forests. Together, we will explore the places of peak happiness, health and abundance – and catch a glimpse into how they came to be that way.

Because whether you are suffering in a failed country or curious about how much better things could be, you deserve to live in Utopia.

 To learn more about the book, scan the code or visit amazon.com/dp/B0BT8HGVQV.

Love Your Life Workbook

The Love Your Life Workbook makes the advice of scientists, researchers, psychologists and physicians more accessible, affordable and actionable. So you can practice tried and tested techniques to create happiness and fulfilment.

The Love Your Life Workbook was designed to help you:

- Tap into happiness – Step into the shoes of your ideal self by finding purpose and rediscovering simple pleasures
- Unlock motivation – Audit your time and redesign your days to hack the habits you want the most and create a foolproof plan to meet your goals
- Build emotional resilience – Generate the ultimate coping master list and turn around your worst days
- Develop meaningful relationships – Become a conversation virtuoso who can manage confrontation like a pro, play the dating game to win and make relationships last like never before

Whether you want to feel more joy every day or feel stronger in times of struggle, the Love Your Life Workbook will help you press the accelerator on your journey towards a life you love.

To learn more about the book, scan the code or visit amazon.com/dp/B09Y5VVN48.

BIBLIOGRAPHY

 Access links to every book, journal, video and article referenced in *Changemaker* by visiting the webpage www.cheatsheets.life/index.php/change or by scanning this code.

ABOUT THE AUTHOR

Ayesha S. Ratnayake (MBA, Chartered Marketer) has over 10 years of experience in marketing and management. A Sri Lankan based in Colombo, Ayesha was born in Suva, Fiji. She has served as CEO, Director and Shareholder of a technology firm where she led the development of an enterprise software product. She has also served as Co-founder and Director of a marketing communications agency. She is a startup mentor, mental health advocate, and the author of *Changemaker*, *The Utopia Playbook*, *Cheat Sheets for Life*, and the *Love Your Life Workbook*. You can contact her at hi@cheatsheets.life.

"Never doubt that a small group of thoughtful,
committed individuals can change the world.
In fact, it's the only thing that ever has."
Margaret Mead

Made in the USA
Columbia, SC
05 September 2024

0f76e9c3-583e-471c-b8d9-b885635ef301R01